THE LOST GARDENS OF HELIGAN

Lovingly created by successive generations of the Tremayne family, in the summer of 1914 Heligan was at its zenith when tragedy struck. More than half its twenty-two gardeners were to fall on the fields of Flanders over the next few years. Its walled gardens and pleasure grounds slowly fell to sleep under mountains of bramble, ivy and rampant laurel and its once celebrated acres became no more than a footnote in history.

Seventy years later, Tim Smit and John Nelson hacked their way through the green shroud that covered Heligan. Captivated by its air of mystery and gentle melancholy, they embarked on a quest that was to change their lives forever.

'Heligan ... is the garden restoration of the century and the place to know about' *George Plumptre, The Times*

'Our most recommended garden' *Gardening Which?*

'Bravo Heligan' *Sir Roy Strong, Mail on Sunday*

'Garden of the Year' *Good Guide to Britain 1999*

Tim Smit was born in 1954 in Scheveningen, Holland, and educated in the UK. After graduating from Durham University he worked as a county archaeologist before spending ten years as a record producer and composer, successful in Europe, the USA and Japan.

In 1987 he and his family moved to Cornwall where, with John Nelson, he was to discover Heligan.

Tim Smit's other major interest is the Eden Project, a scheme to build the largest greenhouse on earth in Cornwall, to celebrate the millennium.

For more information contact:
The Lost Gardens of Heligan
Heligan
Pentewan
St Austell
Cornwall
PL26 6EN
Tel: 01726 845100
Fax: 01726 845101
Website: www.heligan.com; email: info@heligan.com

THE
LOST GARDENS
OF
HELIGAN

Tim Smit

INDIGO

An Indigo paperback
First published in Great Britain by Victor Gollancz in 1997
Revised edition first published in 1999
This new paperback edition published in 2000 by Indigo,
an imprint of Orion Books Ltd,
Orion House, 5 Upper St Martin's Lane,
London WC2H 9EA

A CIP catalogue record for this book is available from the
British Library.

ISBN: 0 57540 245 8

Printed in Great Britain by
The Guernsey Press Co. Ltd, Guernsey, C. I.

For
CANDY
ALEX, LAURA *and* SAM
*Thank you for enduring
– to use Sam's phrase – 'hell again'*

Dedicated
to the memory of
LIZ KNIGHTS
&
Donald Cross
&
Douglas Holland

CONTENTS

PART 3: ACTS OF MEN

Foreword

If, like me, it is only among the windswept Pens and Tres that you're sure you have some Cornish ancestry, you will feel at home at Heligan. It will also help if you have contracted sub-tropical lunacy and can't resist flirting with the sort of plants common-sense gardeners avoid. Dorset can't truly rival Cornwall for mildness, but here, on this extreme westward fringe of the county, we are far from proof against the botanical sirens.

Heligan is a modern miracle. Once the estate of the Tremayne family, its ancient community was definitively scuppered – like so much else – by the First World War. It lost the great bulk of its staff and its thousand acres or more lapsed into almost complete decay. What you are now seeing here is less a fascinating garden – though it remains handsomely that – than the almost archaeological resurrection of a concept, a way of life most of us have only read about; the world of an affluent country house and all it would once have needed in terms of trees and flowers for pleasure, to say nothing of the accompanying vegetable riches – its pineapples, peaches, melons, grapes, kiwis and the rest. Above all Heligan provides a dazzlingly *real* experience of a lost way of life, almost of something from the world of science fiction. It will make even the least imaginative dream.

It needed a thoroughly unusual pair of men to make the dream real for the rest of us. This last November I was (alas, an invalid) being wheeled around the estate by one of them, Tim Smit, who is a main bubbling source of this quite extraordinary product of enterprise, energy and inventiveness. Tim first came here in 1990 – he is Dutch, his mother English – as a successful composer and musical entrepreneur, extraordinarily enough with (then) little botanical knowledge. Everything including the famous tree ferns was so totally sunk in a wild undergrowth of laurels, rhododendrons and brambles that it was almost literally invisible, a true ghost . . . as this book vividly recounts. But Tim and his colleague, the builder John Nelson, fell headlong in love with the remarkable ghost they had unearthed. Perhaps no mere garden lover would have had the endless persistence, or the skill at soliciting and begging, that they developed. I asked Tim what had been the fuse for the superhuman energy they had found. His answer was surprisingly simple and Christian: 'Redemption.' They have clearly been splendidly backed by a number of their helpers and a variety of experts in their own fields. I met some of these on my wheel round. They gave a strong sense of a team, almost a family, sure of what they are doing. By Tim's account many, from all walks of life, have saved the garden by having been themselves first 'saved' by it, by the shame of its desuetude. At one point he said he loathed 'history in aspic'. Oddly there are rumours of people 'seeing strange things'. I could believe that the Tremaynes and their well-to-do guests might happily now return and haunt their ancient domain. The present one does begin to suggest the happy ambience of immemorial order, balance and contentment, the truly good rural society, enshrined in Voltaire's garden.

Of course that was always partly a myth. I can only say that Tim, unphilosophical figure though he may seem, feels close to recreating it. Years ago and not far from here I had to train intending Marine commandos. Ghosts from that remote past appeared as we went round. I sensed myself in the hands of that rarest of all types, the resolute and resourceful commando leader.

Heligan already deeply merits a visit from anyone aware of the vital symbolism of gardens. Tim's new dream is to erect a huge covered garden near St Austell, to show the inter-relationship of all plants and all men. If the Eden Project becomes real, as he hopes it will by the millennium, a visit to this paradisiacal corner of Cornwall will be momentous and essential, something beyond mere silicon valleys and the slick gimmickries of the rest of the world.

John Fowles
November 1996

Acknowledgements

I remember surfacing from the bottom of a flooded clay pit in October 1987 after a diving accident, which I had feared might do me in, and feeling disappointed that my life hadn't flashed in front of me – or if it had, nothing of note had occurred during the course of it. However, since 1990 Heligan has been an important part of my life and writing this book has brought back many happy memories (so I hope this doesn't mean that I'm in imminent danger of meeting my maker). The restoration has attracted more than its fair share of larger-than-life characters and I feel privileged to have shared this time with them. When it comes to thanking people, I feel an irresistible urge to go gooey, like an actor at the Oscars, but the pleasure of recognition is tempered by the worry that I might, through a momentary lapse, forget somebody and spoil things.

I shall start with the book itself. Sue Pring and her husband, Geoff, have helped beyond the call of duty from the earliest days and now Sue's research, early photographs and lovely maps are evident throughout the book. Building on the material offered to us by local historian Ivor Herring, she has been invaluable as a fearless critic. I first met Diane Barrall when she came to Heligan on a BTCV holiday; she went on to do her degree thesis on Heligan and recently helped me to fill in some gaps in research for the book. I would like to express my appreciation to Penelope Willis (née Tremayne), who generously allowed me to use the unpublished early memoirs of John Tremayne (Squire 1851–1901) and shared fond memories of her uncle, Jack, with me. I am indebted to Sue Williamson, Tab Anstice, Damaris Tremayne, Sarah Stokes, Charity Rowlandson and Colin Tyler for allowing me to use their archive photographs to help bring Heligan's past to life.

I would like to thank Susanna Yager of Channel 4 for steering me through the genteel world of publishing. Mike Petty persuaded me to sign to Gollancz and then cajoled me through five months of writing. A perfectionist, his early editing did no good to my vanity, but made a great contribution to the readability of the book. His only weakness appears to be an inability to read train timetables. It has been a real pleasure to work with Katrina Whone, also of Gollancz, whose unrelenting appetite for work, attention to detail and incredible patience saw this project safely through to completion. Heartfelt thanks to my brother-in-law, Jim Simpson, for his timely professional advice, and to Deborah Adams for her sharp but painless copy-editing.

My friends Charlie and Mary Webster will remember their summer holiday at Treveague in 1990, when we stayed up till the small hours putting the finishing touches to Heligan's first planning application. 1996 has seen the venue and the roles reversed, with Candy and me spending many exciting days at College Farm watching the book take shape.

There have also been some lonely, agonizing moments. I would like to thank Stuart Thompson, Paul Travers and John Crawshaw, all of whom bore the brunt of my despair at 'the Lost Chapter of Heligan', which was swallowed whole by my computer at 2 a.m. and never regurgitated, despite all their best efforts. To them should be added Kary Lescure, Jo Stuart Thompson and Wendy Brewin, who have spent hours on fax machines beyond the call of duty.

This book is a celebration of the restoration as a whole, and I make no apology for extending my appreciation to include all those who have taken part, for without them there would have been no story to tell. First, John and Katharine Willis and Damaris Tremayne. Second, our main grant funders, Dr Stewart Harding of the Countryside Commission, George Musgrave of the Rural Development Commission and Nigel Mathews of Cornwall County Council. Their funds were matched by the generosity of more than sixty corporate sponsors, too many to name here so a general thank you will, I hope, suffice. Third, our advisers Philip McMillan Browse and Peter Thoday (who also gave technical advice for the book – Peter, I hope you enjoyed the opera); and Dominic Cole and our mentor and good friend Major Tony Hibbert of Trebah Gardens.

Thank you to the residents of Heligan House and our other neighbours for their support. I must also mention the volunteers, too numerous to name, who have helped us from the early days. George Crumpler and Jean Griffiths of the BTCV have led many teams here and have become firm friends along the way. I would also like to thank Peter Stafford, who has taken Heligan by the scruff of the neck and shaken it into what passes for organization, while I have swanned around pretending to be a writer.

My debt to my friend and partner John Nelson will be obvious to all who read this book. I would find it impossible adequately to describe his importance to Heligan other than perhaps to say that he embodies the spirit of Heligan itself.

Last, but definitely not least, I would like to thank my wife, Candy, the person without whom this book would never have been written and many of whose best ideas have been shamelessly stolen and purveyed as my own. She has drawn together the huge collection of photographs and read and improved hundreds of pages of my writing, distilling it to what I hope you will now enjoy.

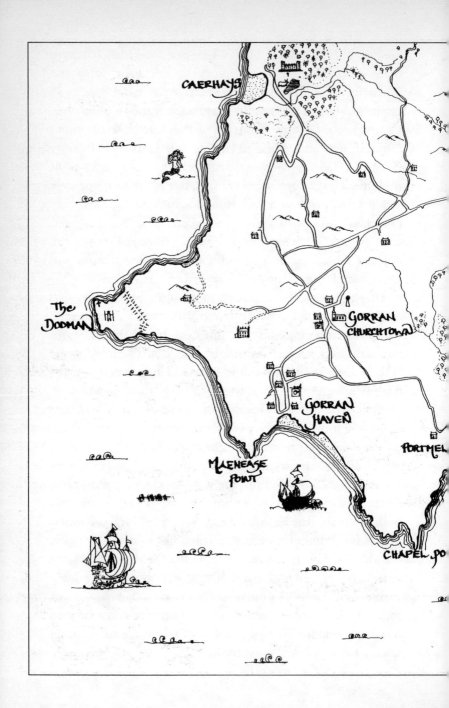

CAERHAYS

The DODMAN

GORRAN CHURCHTOWN

GORRAN HAVEN

MAENEASE POINT

PORTMEL

CHAPEL PO

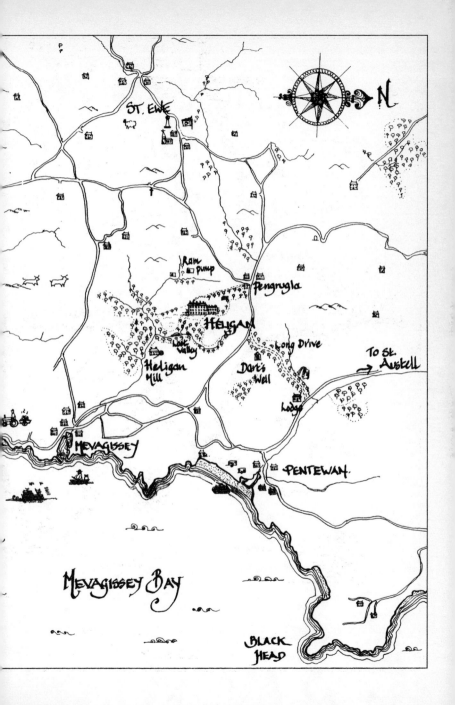

THE NORTHERN GARDENS

(50mm = 100 metres)

1 The Mount
2 Flora's Green
3 The Ride
4 Northern Summerhouse
5 Vegetable Garden
6 The Ravine
7 New Zealand
8 Crystal Grotto and
  Wishing Well
9 Cornish Apple Orchard
10 Bee-bole lawn

11 Melon Garden
12 Italian Garden
13 Head Gardener's
  Office
14 Banana House
15 Reserve Garden
16 Poultry Yard
17 Peach House
18 Vinery
19 Flower Garden
20 Sundial Garden

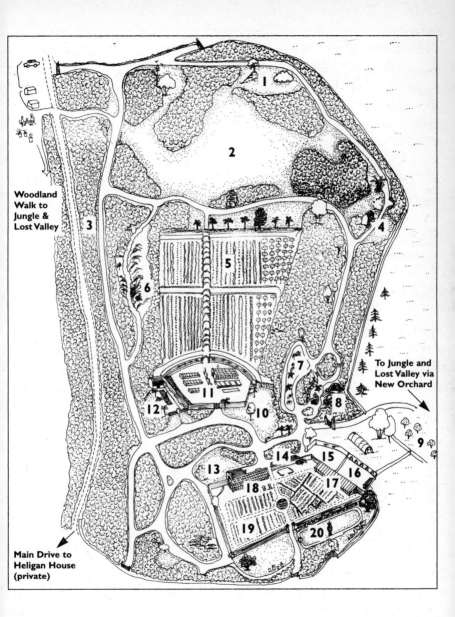

Woodland
Walk to
Jungle &
Lost Valley

To Jungle and
Lost Valley via
New Orchard

Main Drive to
Heligan House
(private)

THE JUNGLE &
THE LOST VALLEY

(15mm = 100 metres)

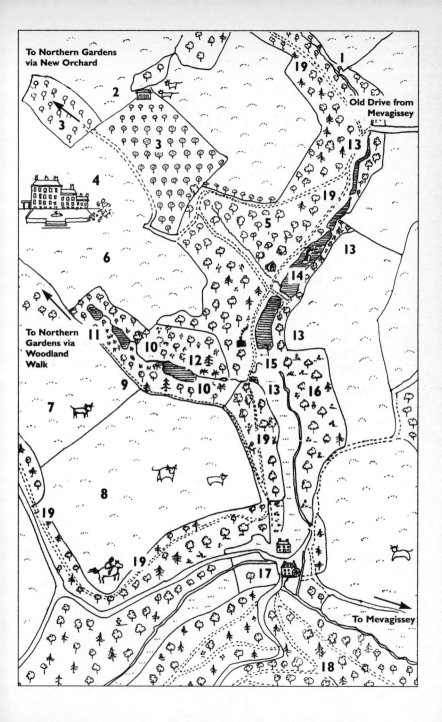

To Northern Gardens
via New Orchard

2

3

4

6

To Northern
Gardens via
Woodland
Walk

11

10

12

9

10

7

8

19

19

19

13

5

14

13

13

15

13

16

19

17

18

Old Drive from
Mevagissey

13

19

To Mevagissey

THE
LOST GARDENS
OF
HELIGAN

Introduction

THE GREEN
SHROUD

It was the silence, the unearthly silence that struck you first. Some silences have a stillness to them, a calm that suggests a moment of life at rest, but this was a silence that vested everything with a deep, brooding melancholy. Gradually, it dawned on you: you could hear no birdsong, no rustlings, nor even the far-off murmur of life elsewhere. Even the wind seemed to hold its breath, the only sound a faint and distant creaking, like the settling timbers of a ship at anchor.

This dank, dark place had its own strange beauty. We had cut our way through what we later discovered had once been a formal laurel hedge, grown to shield the pleasure grounds from those who had used the main drive to the big house. The hedge had grown massive and now stretched at least thirty yards in width. Here, in this underworld, the laurel trunks arched and writhed, contorted into a Medusa's fringe of unimaginable shapes. I had never seen such boughs before. It wasn't just their size, though that was impressive enough, some of the main stems being thicker than a big man's thigh. It was also the velvety feel of them, like new stag's horn. Starved of sun for so long, they played host to legions of algae in a startling palette of colours, from lime green through orange to blue-black.

Having crawled on hands and knees, climbed, cut, pulled and pushed our way through to the far side of the hedge, we had to let our eyes adjust to the daylight and reflect on the sight that greeted us. There were brambles snaking everywhere. Thickly matted to chest height, they ensnared all the trees and shrubs, at times seeming to defy gravity as they arched across open space like angel hair on a Christmas tree. Poking through this sea of thorns were some amazing plants; huge rhododendrons, what appeared to be palm trees, indeterminate evergreens, all framed by massive, still living trees keeled over like drunks.

I had never given much thought to brambles before, except when blackberry picking. You could not help but admire the pioneering spirit of the plant, its shading so successful that none but the hardiest of competitors could thrive in what little light it left behind. Underneath its blanket was the stench of decay, the only survivors shade-loving ferns and those plants that were tall enough to escape its hungry embrace and reach for the sun. In most cases even they were disfigured, looking like tall tribesmen with rickety legs and big hair.

We exercised the greatest caution as we cut our way through the unending bramble patch, punctuated by what appeared to be an avenue of palm trees with a line of tall evergreens as a backcloth. The oldest brambles were woody and as thick as your thumb, and quite capable of inflicting serious injury on the unwary. A too-casual sweep of the machete could lead to it bouncing off, or the bramble snapping with a sound like a whiplash and flashing past your face, leaving you to reflect humbly on the importance of your eyesight.

Our plan was to cut from one side to the other so as to give ourselves a sense of scale for what we were looking at. In due course we found ourselves at the foot of an enormous oak tree, where at last the brambles began to relent. In the bole of the tree we heard a low humming, which was unusual in itself. We peered up, to be transfixed by the sight of the most enormous wasps I have ever had the misfortune to come across. To my phobic imagination they were at least two inches long and looked like evil incarnate.

We found good reasons to hurry away from this place, and plunged through some straggly laurels to find ourselves on what might have been a path; by looking up at the sky, we could make out an avenue of palms and rhododendrons through which our route meandered. We cut our way through with renewed vigour, only to find our path blocked by a massive tree, its trunk at least six feet across. It was still alive, its branches apparently impenetrable. As we inched along it we could just make out exotic fern-like plants and a tantalizing, brilliant flash of colour from an early-flowering rhododendron. But we couldn't get through.

I had only just met John Willis, but this moment created the bond. In desperation we retraced our steps with the idea of finding a new route round the tree. As we hurried John remarked that there appeared to be a stone edging underfoot. All of a sudden we could see what looked like a rockery, its rough-hewn stones crowned with enormous rhododendrons and the exotic fern-like plants we'd seen in the glade beyond the fallen tree. We were drawn down the path and found ourselves back in deep shade, descending what must once have been steps, although they were buried well beneath the debris. We kept our balance by holding on to the rockery stones which led, to our amazement, to the mouth of a cave. Its beautifully corbelled entrance arch was veiled by drooping laurel branches growing out of the roof. Inside it was wet and cold, the walls and ceiling covered in mould. A curved stone bench seat lined the wall, most of it buried under a thick cushion of loam. This was obviously a trysting spot of old . . . or were we being hopelessly romantic?

Beyond the cave the narrow path meandered through a range of moss-covered rockeries until we came upon a well, set into the face of one of them. It was flooded, and what appeared to be an ornate Gothic capstone lay face down in the water in front of it. The whole structure was simply built and covered in moss, giving it the appearance of great age.

We walked on from the well, ducked under some fallen trees and found ourselves looking, bizarrely, at a modern hardcore road, driven through with no concern for the plants. Piles of earth, splintered trees and shrubs, a mountain of debris; whoever had done this had no idea that there was a garden here at all. We traced the entire route and found that it cut from the main drive through to parkland. It was nothing more than a farm track.

The spell was broken, and we were all set to retrace our steps back to the real world. But something else caught our attention. From the track we could make out, through mountainous rhododendrons, the outline of a structure. On drawing closer we could see a large brick wall with what must once have been working buildings set against it. They were mostly gutted, their timbers rotten, yet these ruins had a resonance, an all-pervading sense of sadness, that captivated the imagination. Gingerly, not wishing to bring the walls down, we crept into one of them and found, behind some fallen roof slates, an old stokehole, with a boiler set at the bottom of a flight of steps. A doorway led into a tiny room with a broken window and a fireplace, inside which we could still make out the kettle-hooks. Poking out from under the debris was the old kettle, rusted and knobbly with the accretions of years spent waiting for its next call to service.

Back outside, our spirits much lifted, we faced the ruins of a glasshouse of unlikely proportions, so small one couldn't imagine being able to grow anything in it whatsoever. Next to it was a large wooden door that led, we supposed, to the other side of the great wall. It was slightly ajar, and yet more of the indefatigable brambles could be seen through the holes in its rotten panels. Wild horses could not have stopped us pushing that door open. It squealed and groaned, but by rocking it gently to and fro we eased a gap big enough to squeeze through, back into the impenetrable undergrowth.

It was an unforgettable moment. Close in front of us we could see the finial of a glasshouse gable-end at a crazy angle, like a sinking ship. To our right was the door into another glasshouse. Most of the glass was broken, and what remained was of a curious size and shape, but by peering in we could make out that it was the start of a range that carried on until the all-embracing brambles obscured the view. Cast-iron heating pipes snaked into the distance, tempting us to follow.

Only on turning the rusty door handle did we realize the danger. A small push, and there was the sudden sound of crashing glass. We looked up to see that the whole glasshouse had slipped from the top of the wall and was supported only by the doorframe and the bramble twisting through its cross-members. What little glass that remained was just lying there; the wooden lights which framed it had rotted out years ago. Any sudden movement could have brought it all down, with us underneath. We would have to cut our way around the front of the houses if we were to see what was on the other side. Here we discovered that the door had been the entrance to a matched pair of houses which led into a larger glasshouse with a higher roof and its own entrance from the opposite end. This house seemed to have withstood time's ravages better than the others. Its door gave way with a little screech, and we were in.

The watery morning sun had finally burnt off the clouds, and its dappled light filled the house, giving it a church-like air. A web of brambles choked everything from floor to ceiling. An image of them as nature's stormtroopers came to mind. A garden is a symbol of man's arrogance, perverting nature to human ends; perhaps the brambles were exacting retribution for this vanity by giving a powerful demonstration of the transience of all things.

Just when I was in danger of becoming seriously depressed by these notions of death and decay I spotted a leaf that didn't look much like a bramble and followed its branch back to the stem. It was a vine, and an old vine at that. Looking up, I could distinguish it weaving in and out of the broken panes along the whole length of the building. There in the midst of all this decay was another, far more powerful symbol – that of regeneration. Perhaps I have an unusually optimistic nature, but I felt hugely excited by this image of resurgence. My eye was drawn to something hanging on the wall: a small pair of rusty scissors, presumably for cutting grapes. How long had they been there? Who did they belong to? What was their story? What had happened here?

A chap can only take so much of this Indiana Jones stuff, and a pint of bitter beckoned. John and I, wearied by our morning's explorations, decided to go out the easy way, along the farm track. But I knew then that I was enchanted, and that this was more than just a boyish enthusiasm.

What follows is a personal chronicle of the unlikely train of events that first brought me to Heligan, and of what happened thereafter. As the history of this extraordinary place began to unravel, it quickly became clear that academic research alone would not reveal the whole picture. Heligan rapidly became an obsession occupying every waking hour, to the exclusion of almost everything else. I will never forget how John Willis and I came upon the garden and how its atmosphere struck a chord with us. Since then, although we have readily sought the advice of every relevant specialist, if ever we have doubted a course of action – even if scientifically, horticulturally, economically or legally correct – our actions have been measured against what Heligan itself insisted upon.

Set in a magical place, this is a romantic adventure story, not an academic tome. We have spent the last five years thinking on our feet, eating on the hoof . . . and always with our hearts pounding in our chests. And yes, we have breathed new life back into the gardens, but every breath has made us feel more alive too. Anyone who has visited Heligan will understand. It is a story of teamwork and passion, of people with disparate lives coming together and sharing a common goal. It is a story which celebrates that which is best in us all, commitment, compassion and a love of life.

Part One
ACT OF GOD

Chapter 1

THE BIG BLOW

In October 1987 we had had what you might call a bit of a
practice run. We lived in a solid brick-built Victorian
terraced house in Brixton, South London – witness to many
a rich and colourful experience over time no doubt, but not
prone to natural disasters. Our experience of parenthood
had reached its zenith in terms of sleep deprivation, and we
had become used to killing the small hours rocking fretful
babies, standing at the bay window in our bedroom,
watching the urban night life; foxes raiding the dustbins and
the occasional minor fracas on the street. But that night,
from nowhere, suddenly you could see the wind, swirling,
biting, cutting down the road. It seemed to make no fuss, not
bothering with clattering, banging, and finally raising the bin
lids to scatter them against the twin walls of parked cars. It
simply blew . . . all through the night while many slumbered
unaware.

The next morning some of our closest friends were literally trapped in their houses by fallen trees. Some climbed out
of upstairs windows, while others waited for the Fire Brigade
to arrive with its rescue equipment, a paltry issue of hand
axes. I explored the devastated areas nearby with a neighbour
who had a chainsaw. It was a wonderful opportunity to fill
his woodshed whilst providing a service to the community,

helping to reopen a major route through our capital city. (Later I was to remember how impressed I had been with this comparatively simple machine.) Clapham Common had witnessed a late-night session of giants playing nine-pins and, further afield, the renowned Sevenoaks had lost all but two. Many of our favourite haunts, among them Sheffield Park and Scotney Castle, would never be the same again. We had already made arrangements to leave the big smoke, and all its memories, for pastures new, and the Big Blow seemed a fitting way to end an era.

For generations my wife Candy's family had holidayed in Cornwall, and I grew to love it too. During a trip in 1987, we spontaneously made an offer on a house and to our amazement sold our home in Brixton a fortnight later.

Treveague was not objectively ideal, out on an isolated limb the 'wrong' side of Exeter and near the crest of a constantly windswept hill. But from the first moment we found it utterly compelling. You could breathe the fresh air deep into your lungs and feel your soul reviving. Its posse of upstairs windows all faced the south-easterly sunshine, but each framed its own unique view of an idyllic old orchard, and a valley stretching as far as we could crane our necks, down the grassy path in everyone's mind's eye, to a blue and beckoning bay. The house itself triggered all sorts of memories of special places in the homes of all our grandparents: slate shelves in an old dairy, secret passages, back staircases with the remnants of bells to call the staff . . . the musty smell of history lingering into the present. While we were aware of the subjective nature of these sensations, the feeling of belonging was real enough; and leaving London was no longer an issue, simply a foregone conclusion.

The circumstances in which we found Treveague were a sign of the times. A wonderful old family-run farm had been forced into fragmentation, and we sidestepped in our minds the fact that our purchase had sealed its fate. It was for us to offer the continuity of care and to encourage the development of a new community. Deep stuff – and, as it turned out, psychological preparation for far greater challenges.

When we moved into our new home, in torrents of rain and a week before Christmas, we were barely prepared for everything that lay ahead, although we were well equipped with enthusiasm and determination. The early days were a catalogue of disasters, designed to test our resolve. As professionally predicted, we lived amongst rubble for months, innocently greeting each new day as it dawned with uncharted adventures ahead. A team of fascinated builders uncovered a range of thrills before our breakfast table and we ended up with five options for preparing a meal: a mud hearth with iron spikes to hang the pots; a clay clome bread oven set adjacent to the main flue, a Victorian range made in St Austell; an inter-war Rayburn to provide the luxury of hot water without which it would have been hard to sustain the spirits, and finally – our only contribution to the services – an electric cooker which my granny had acquired second hand in the sixties.

Soon after we moved into Treveague, we pulled out a small modern fireplace in the living room, and to our amazement uncovered a massive walk-in hearth, with a view clear to the sky, the flue so wide a grown man could have climbed to the top of the chimney from the inside in comfort. Excitement turned to alarm when we noticed that the whole chimney was supported by what had once been a massive oak lintel, which now seemed to be composed of little more than dust. A cursory prod with a penknife confirmed our worst fears when it sank in up to the hilt. And so it was in a condition of blind panic that I was first to meet John Nelson, a local builder and one of my future partners in the project to restore Heligan Gardens. He came with a reputation for restoration work on old and historic houses. Ours, being old, fitted the bill; and but for John could easily have become historic in the wrong sense of the word. He came to our rescue and, with a flashing smile that oozed confidence, and fuelled by enormous quantities of tea, he and his team of hefty chaps braced everything and replaced the rotten lintel with a large beam of seasoned oak, found skulking at the back of a local reclamation yard.

One January morning in 1990 dawned a particularly unenthusiastic grey, and for want of distraction we uncharacteristically tuned in to the radio news. It warned of a severe storm approaching; the schools were closed, and the advice was to stay at home. Suddenly the house was shuddering and the lights went out. I found some batteries and we tuned in to the radio once more, tracing the course of the devastation. With our hatches battened down as best I could, the initial overriding need to stick with this storm-tossed vessel gave way, in the ensuing hours, to a desperate urge to abandon ship. The hurricane was terrifying as it tore our home apart in broad daylight, with our young family inside. Slates crashed from the roof in sheets around our ears, and while the sash windows could only fretfully rattle and bang, those on hinges worked the bolts loose and one of our new french windows was ripped from its frame and took off into the garden. With the old latches still unrepaired on many of the internal doors, the hurricane now swept unimpeded into our house via the sitting room and swirled in gusts up the main staircase and into our bedroom. Candy, immobilized in bed after a wisdom tooth operation the day before, stayed under the covers, marshalling a hopeless plan of action and reporting further losses. Some days later the fever from infection would render her delirious; the doctor was summoned to give her antibiotics and about the same time our electricity finally returned. The structural repairs to the house would take a lot longer.

As the weeks passed, life resumed its usual course amid a manageable state of chaos. Three upstairs rooms were sealed off with collapsed ceilings, and of an evening our home resembled a field hospital with bodies on mattresses strewn across any available floorspace. Treveague had not taken the full force of the hurricane alone. Our experiences were typical of much of the South West. I had seen a complete mobile home leap over a hedge and shatter into smithereens in the field beyond. However, in spite of its exposed position, the surrounding farm appeared to have taken minimal damage, largely because previous blows over the decades had already picked off any unstable or top-heavy structures in the area. Our farmhouse was repairable, and after considerable regrouping we called in the builders to make a start.

On close inspection, it was discovered that the huge Elizabethan chimney at the west end of our farmhouse had developed a crack. This was particularly serious because it was held together by lime mortar which, once shifted, had become unstable. At any moment twenty feet of chimney could have come piling down through our far bedroom, taking most of the middle of the house with it.

In this new emergency there was obviously only one man for the job. In no time at all we had scaffolding up the side of the building and around the chimney. One of John's mates, Dave Burns, who had developed a good head for heights after many years working in the merchant navy, scaled the lofty platform to photograph the detail of the chimney before painstakingly, brick by brick, it was taken down to the wallplate and made safe; and a plastic sheet covered the hole while we decided what to do. We were in a real pickle because the house had been 'listed' soon after we had moved in and that meant we were obliged to reinstate all original external features exactly as we had found them.

Unable to use the original bricks, or find any substitutes locally, I decided to hire a van and go on a tour of South London reclamation yards, where there was such a concentration of brick that I would be bound to find a match. After several attempts, I found what I was looking for, promptly loaded up three tons of bricks and headed for home on the M4. It was Bank Holiday Monday and I was looking forward to showing John the bricks. He was bound to be impressed.

Some people feel guilty at the sight of a blue light. Years of living in Brixton cured me of that, which must explain why I failed to notice the police motorcyclists trying to flag me down. I eventually stopped and they were angry and unmoved by my broken Dutch routine, ordering me to follow them off at Junction 18. I was made to drive the van over a weighbridge and an inspector called me into an office and informed me that I had the biggest percentage axle overload ever recorded on a vehicle. Apparently a three-ton van isn't meant to carry that weight, let alone on pallets over the axles. There would be a trip to court and a massive fine of probably £5000. To make matters worse, I would have to unload the vehicle there and then if I wanted to use it to return home. I called John Nelson in desperation and he told me to hang on while he found a lorry. Four hours or so later he showed up having found one and driven it two hundred miles to help. 'No such thing as a problem,' he said, as he began to load the bricks by hand. Somehow, in his company, you believed it.

I've always had a soft spot for pigs. Quite why I'm not sure, but I have a recollection of sitting under one of those naive Victorian farmyard paintings in a pub in Durham, marvelling at the unlikely physical proportions of the beast and feeling that this was my sort of animal. This general admiration would never have translated itself into ownership but for a quirk of fate, which, like so many things over the next few years, was going to change my life for ever. In 1989, out of the blue, I had received a phone call from Rob Poole, the director of Newquay Zoo. Cramped for space, he was looking to find foster homes for some of his animals.

'Would you like a Vietnamese pot-bellied pig? In fact, I've got a breeding pair.' Silence. 'They're very friendly, have small appetites and, unlike other pigs, they don't root about damaging the land ... They're very clean, in fact they're so clean many people keep them as house pets.'

'Oh really?'

'Can I take that as a yes?'

One evening, some time after this, a small van pulling a hutch-like trailer drew up outside the farmhouse. Rob Poole had come in person to hand over his precious cargo. Greetings over, the trailer was ceremonially opened and its contents decanted. It has to be said that a pot-bellied pig's face is not its fortune. The words 'accident' and 'brick wall' come instantly to mind. However, I loved them (for there were two) on sight. Already christened Horace and Doris, they became instant local celebrities, famed as much for their great ugliness as for their grumpiness. Their home, a shed in the field behind the farmhouse, became a point of pilgrimage for all those walking the public footpath which goes past our door. There was one serious minus point, which Rob had neglected to mention: they snored. They snored like rumbling volcanoes. In fact they snored so loudly and deeply that you could feel the ground shake. It was to be many nights before we adjusted to this new background noise.

Rob was Falstaffian, a big man in every sense. He wore T-shirts in sub-zero temperatures and his massive forearms always bore the scars of the latest fracas he'd had with one of his charges. A bottomless reservoir of enormously funny and unlikely stories, and a talent for making an hour turn into an evening without your noticing, made Rob wonderful company. This was mixed with the patience of Job, which I put down to his lifelong experience of working with animals, and a spectacular temper – which he reserved for humans. In short, Rob was slightly larger than life ... and he dedicated himself to getting the most out of it. I was later to discover that this quest took many strange forms. He could spend hours tinkering with the recipes of his home brews, which enjoyed a fearsome reputation not only for their ability to deliver a hangover without the necessity of getting drunk, but also for their explosive qualities. His kitchen could have been an alchemist's den: there were always dozens of barrels, bottles and pickling jars and every beam had something potentially edible or drinkable hanging from it. Rob was a man in whose company it was not possible to be thirsty, hungry ... or bored.

This did not stop *Rob* being bored. Once satisfied that the pigs were comfortable, and that I fully understood all their requirements and knew what to do in emergencies, we settled down over a drink. Despite Rob's love of animals and loyalty to the zoo, he felt that its days were numbered and found that he couldn't easily square its necessary role as an entertainment – after all, the entrance money kept the zoo open – with the genuine needs of conservation. Newquay Zoo at that time bore all the hallmarks of having been designed by architects on secondment from the prison service. While you couldn't deny that the cages had a certain bunker chic, capable of withstanding a full frontal military assault, they were quite out of proportion to the needs of some rather small monkeys, and the protection of the fingers of little children.

I found it strange that Rob had never travelled to the far-flung corners of the earth to see his animals in their natural habitats. In fact, in all the time I knew him, he never once expressed any desire to do so. His main passion in life was closer to home, where a keen interest in native flora and fauna had developed into a concern for the future of rare breed farm animals, and the impact of their decline on the world of agriculture. Indeed at home he had a collection of rare poultry and kept Tamworth pigs with which he used to wrestle as a hobby. Although our conversation meandered all over the place, it kept coming back to rare breeds and ecologically balanced farming. While the idea of starting a serious rare breeds farm gained an ever-increasing hold on our imaginations, as do most great ideas explored over a bottle, I very much doubt that either of us truly believed it would prove to be anything more than a fantasy, a game of make-believe that would have found an echo in a million similar conversations around the world on any night you care to mention.

As the hurricane of January 1990 subsided and dusk approached, it seemed little short of a miracle to find our new litter of Vietnamese pot-bellied pigs, born to Horace and Doris in our neighbours' barn, suckling peacefully in the straw under a hurricane lamp and blissfully unaware of the turmoil around them.

Soon afterwards, a letter arrived. Rob Poole wanted to know whether I had been serious about starting a rare breeds farm. If so, could we have a talk? I called him and he agreed to come over. It was the end of a long day. The chimney was almost finished and it had got to the hairy bit, when the massive chimney-pot had to be raised to the top of the scaffold and put in place. John was not too keen on heights, so he had brought in his son, Steve, to help. We were all down in the kitchen mulling over the problem with another brew of tea, when a big head appeared round the door, sporting a huge grin and a number one haircut of almost penal severity.

As Rob and I began discussing a suitable location for our venture, it became clear that we had engaged John's interest and he offered a few suggestions. He had a passion for collecting mushrooms, which had led him to cover almost every inch of the countryside and gained him extensive local knowledge. We talked for hours, the chimney forgotten. A rare breeds farm would need shelter and water and good quality grazing, and Rob, with all his experience in the tourism industry, was insistent that the site should also be near a main road. The area he favoured was between St Austell and Gorran.

The next afternoon, following up a suggestion from John, Rob and I drove through the gates of Pengrugla campsite posing as potential campers. Rob had two sacks of lion dung in the back of his van that he had promised to someone for use as a deterrent to badgers. Pengrugla was everything we were looking for, although the manager seemed discouragingly settled and buoyant about his future plans. During the course of the conversation he volunteered that he leased the campsite from the local estate.

That evening I wrote a letter to the estate, explaining what we were looking for and why. The response was quick in coming, and I was invited to meet the company secretary for coffee at the Pentewan Sands office.

'Before we go any further, I have to tell you that the

Pengrugla campsite is out of the question. The present tenant has only just taken over and has already begun to invest in it. But I do like your idea.' The man took a heavy pull on a cigarette and spluttered.

'You should quit, it's bad for your health,' I said, lighting a cigar.

'I only started smoking again today. It's national non-smoking day and I won't have anyone lecturing me about what I should and shouldn't do.'

This was my introduction to John Willis, company secretary of Pentewan Sands and, more interestingly, a member of the family who owned the estate. He was younger than me, perhaps in his early thirties, and utterly charming. The conversation widened and eventually he said, 'I'd like to show you something. My sister and I recently inherited some land.'

I cannot in all honesty claim that as we got into John's car I had any expectation whatsoever, other than to spend a couple of hours in good company. A mile up the road there was a derelict garden, now rendered all but inaccessible. The ancient shelter belts, once planted as protection from prevailing winds, had recently stood to face one final winter blast. Massive oaks had come crashing down, unselective of their kill. Had Cornwall's Great Storm of 1990 finally sealed the fate of Heligan – or could it be the trigger for a previously inconceivable recovery? February 16, 1990 was the day I first went with John Willis to explore the lost gardens. In retrospect it was a day that was to change our lives.

That first visit lived on in the conversations around our kitchen table over the ensuing weeks. John Nelson – the builder – massaged my enthusiasm with rumours he had heard of half the present-day population of Mevagissey having been conceived amongst the palms and bamboos of an overgrown tropical valley which connected the fishing village with Heligan. There were tales of temples and poachers finding mosaic floors. Rob's continuing visits, supposedly to discuss the rare breeds project, coincided with these fantastical conversations, until the three of us were helplessly caught up together in a wild plan. With every passing day it seemed to take on a more mythic quality, like a quest, for there is no more powerful or intoxicating force than the awakening of the spirit of adventure.

Part Two

ACTS OF FAITH

Chapter 2

BAPTISM OF FIRE

The White Hart Hotel, St Austell, has the comforting respectability of tweeds and brogues. Hunting prints, leather chairs and liveried staff conjure up images of well-to-do farmers in market day best or mine captains meeting salesmen from 'upcountry'. The smell of filter coffee is the only concession to changing times.

We were there to meet the fearsome Damaris Tremayne. Her reputation, as the matriarch of the Tremayne family, went before her. On numerous occasions John Willis and his sister Antonia had exchanged knowing glances when her name had cropped up in conversation. We hadn't been allowed to meet her earlier, by inference because she had come across spivs like us before and we would be shown the door as soon as good manners allowed.

The Heligan Estate is owned by three separate trusts. The gardens themselves are owned by a trust set up for John and Antonia Willis, who, as the beneficiaries, are able to influence but not dictate which course that trust should take. Such decisions are the job of the trustees. As the senior family member, Damaris saw herself as an intermediary in the trust's affairs. The first hurdle had been a request that we should provide a business plan to demonstrate the viability of our case. Damaris wasn't going to have the estate's good name brought into question by a failed venture, and she wouldn't consider giving us a lease until she was satisfied. We had spent four months working with Graham, my accountant from London, developing our scheme for a garden restoration and rare breeds park to be opened to the public – although he was bitterly opposed to the whole process, saying that it was madness to hand a third party all this information without any certainty of the outcome. I calmed him down and convinced him that John Willis was totally honourable and that there was nothing to fear. So here we were, Graham, Rob, John and Antonia Willis and me, sipping filter coffee and making small talk while we waited for the Arrival.

With film-star timing Damaris swept in and, seating herself at the head of the mahogany-effect conference table, launched into an analysis of the business plan. Though she looked like Margaret Rutherford, all similarity ended there. The first question was a bit of a conversation stopper, about genetic problems in cattle. John and Antonia had failed to warn Rob that Damaris was a respected cattle judge. Having winched up his jaw from the floor, Rob answered with all the composure he could muster. Damaris had also noticed a reference to one of our potential partners as being 'at the cutting edge of animal husbandry' – and a waspish question about the sharpness of his razor blades consigned him to the dustbin of history.

It was my turn next. Friends of hers owned Pencarrow, a magnificent house with fine gardens near Wadebridge, close to where she lived, and they had barely twenty thousand visitors a year. How did I imagine that a completely derelict garden and parkland, without a house, was going to attract double that figure? It was inconceivable. So much for the business plan. John interceded and made calming noises to his aunt about Rob's experience at Newquay Zoo, and

Damaris relented. While she didn't believe a word of the business plan, she would make a deal with us. If we could get planning permission for our proposal, at no cost to the estate, she would consider a lease. Interview over.

Because of John and Rob's work commitments, it fell to me to start the ball rolling with the planners. They thought the idea was good in principle, but needed evidence that the scheme was financially viable and that the site and local roads could cope with the projected number of visitors. The borough forester wanted reassurances that the fine specimen trees rumoured to be in the grounds would be protected. Plans would need to be drawn up outlining the full extent of our proposal. It would probably take about two months to go through the system, but there were local elections coming soon and this might colour events. A lot would depend on public reaction as candidates could not afford to support anything that might be seen as contentious.

Once he'd seen the gardens Gerry Braine, the borough forester, became as enthusiastic as we were. He introduced me to friends of his, Geoff and Sue Pring, both landscape architects, whose practice had already been commissioned by the Cornwall Gardens Trust to record and survey some of the disappearing gardens of Cornwall for English Heritage. Heligan was on their list.

They arrived promptly, bringing with them a colleague, Mike Westley, to begin laying the foundations of a systematic record, on which the restoration would eventually be based. After a day spent exploring and photographing we discussed our options in the light of our immediate need to secure outline planning permission. Geoff agreed to undertake the work necessary on a 'no fee no foal' basis. The most pressing aspect would be the master plan, including a design for a car park. They would start immediately.

The next few weeks rushed past as I tried to meet all the borough councillors who would have a say in the final decision. George Down, my own local councillor, explained the Byzantine workings of the Planning Committee and set up meetings for me with the other local representatives, and with the chairman and deputy chairman. When I took them individually around the accessible parts of the garden their initial reaction was positive and my confidence grew. I was advised to start talking to all our potential neighbours to make them feel comfortable with the idea, and so I introduced myself to the residents of the Big House, now divided into flats. Though nobody was openly hostile, several were worried about the potential invasion of their privacy.

'What about all them wild animals, how they goin' to stop them gettin' out and causin' problems in Meva, then? We don't want lions or tigers goin' down the high street, do we?'

Where the rumours started God only knows, but start they did. There were two schools of thought. The first involved a cross between Windsor Safari Park and Longleat. The worry here concerned the size and relative ferocity of our animals. Oddly enough, their worst anxiety wasn't the lions, elephants or tigers. It was the crocodiles that we would be keeping in the lakes. If they should escape no one would be safe, especially since they could hide in the sewers.

The second theory sprang from my previous connections with the music industry. This venture was quite obviously a front for something else. Before long we were hearing rumours of sightings of famous musicians, after which embellishment came confirmation that the real plan involved the creation of a site for pop festivals.

Anyone undertaking a project should take notice of

rumour before it gets out of hand. Rob, John and I would hoot with laughter as the ever more implausible tales did the rounds, but stupidly we misjudged the mood of the moment, thinking nobody would take them seriously in the absence of hard evidence. Before long it dawned on us that we had a problem. Planning permission wasn't a foregone conclusion. The councillors weren't sure any more whether they would be able to support us.

When our application came up for consideration in the borough chamber, the planning officer duly stood up and said he could not recommend it. There had been a sea of protest letters and a petition, the Highways Department doubted that the roads could cope, and so the litany went on. Finally one of the councillors suggested that in fairness there should be a site meeting, and to our relief this was voted through. At least we'd live to fight another day – but we were on the ropes.

We had two weeks in which to build a solid case. Even then, with local elections looming, we had our doubts whether we'd get a fair hearing. We had to borrow some money to cover the costs of a first-class planning lawyer to argue the legal minutiae with the planning officer, and Mike Westley would be coming to talk about the landscape aspects of the work, including the design for the all-important car park. The site meeting would take the form of a walk around the garden and parkland, followed by a public meeting at St Ewe Village Hall, where the case would be heard.

August 1, 1990 began and ended as a shambles. No one had arranged any parking spaces at Heligan so people had to park all over the place; up the main drive, on the farm track, as well as on the main road. Nobody took charge, so a great gaggle of people wandered aimlessly about without any properly arranged route or presentation. Many appeared to have come out of curiosity, seizing a unique opportunity to see what lay behind the forbidding gates at the top lodge, with their Keep Out signs and dire warnings to trespassers. Still others were strolling around with ill-concealed disdain on their faces, as if to say that they knew what our real agenda was and weren't taken in. It was a case of warm smiles and poodle-like goodwill versus stony poker faces.

It went from bad to worse. At some stage in the proceedings it was judged to be the right time to adjourn to the Village Hall, but half the party didn't get the message and arrived slightly late fearing that the plot was now well and truly hatched. First one up was the planning officer reiterating his earlier concerns, followed by the man from Highways who said that he felt the roads would be able to take the traffic. He was booed and hissed. Then it was my turn to give our version of the plans. Except for appearing as the witch with the least number of words in *Macbeth*, I'd never spoken in public before (unless you count saying inane things like 'Thank you very much, Amsterdam, you've been a lovely audience,' while on tour with a band years previously), so I was very nervous and it showed. Matters weren't helped by a member of the audience who jeered 'A likely story' and 'If you believe that you'll believe anything' at the end of each sentence I spluttered. Mike Westley faced the baying hordes with all the composure of a rabbit in the headlights of a truck, and by the time our lawyer got up he might as well have been speaking Esperanto for all the attention he was given. Someone then observed, to general bewilderment, that there were more people in the hall than at the original VE Day celebrations. This was followed by an earnest plea from the chairman of the Residents' Committee of Heligan House to spare them the plague of rats which must surely accompany our arrival. Another resident then stood up. In time Ivor Herring would offer his valuable services to the restoration, but on this occasion he was an angry and a worried man. Waving his cane at the assembled multitude, he invoked the powers-that-be to see through this tissue of lies: for the gardens were beyond saving. Our plans were not viable and it was quite obvious that such a venture would end in tears. He then narrowed his eyes, looked meaningfully at the Planning Committee and asked them, in conspiratorial tones, whether they knew what this meant. Being met by blank stares all round, he went on to explain that this was an old ruse. Put in an application for something that will certainly fail and then put in another, later on, for development, on the grounds that the ideal use of the land was demonstrably uneconomic. This theory was greeted with gasps of admiration from all and sundry and we stood there like the naked emperors we so obviously were.

To their credit the Planning Committee announced that they had to retire behind closed doors to deliberate. They ducked into the cramped confines of the kitchen, spoiling the effect slightly by making an immediate return. The banging of a gavel on the trestle table summoned the crowd to order, and in the hushed silence the gardens were praised to the skies and we were proclaimed guilty: sorry, planning permission refused. The throng broke into a roaring tumult of celebration. As I caught the eyes of several of the councillors they shrugged apologetically and disappeared out into the night.

I suppose in our hearts we must have expected it, but it hurt nonetheless and there was a moment when our resolve wobbled. We had none of us experienced such aggression before and we felt quite shaken by it. John Willis, who had come to the meeting, invited our team back to his house on Pentewan beach for a drink to drown our sorrows.

★

Perhaps the most important aspect of democracy is that you can take nothing for granted. In order to carry people with you, they must be kept fully informed and criticism has to be anticipated and answered before it is voiced. Everyone must play their part. When inaction is deemed to signify approval and action – ironically – associated with opposition, democracy can easily be subverted by a minority. The opponents of a plan will write and draw up petitions because of the strength of their feelings; supporters believe their view is being championed anyway and so remain silent. This leaves the authorities no choice but to state that the majority of the views expressed to them have been negative. Anyone leading a project must organize their support accordingly.

Rob Poole, John Nelson and I faced up to our immediate problems. If we were to succeed with a revised application, the first item on our agenda had to be the rare breeds park. It was obvious that this was regarded as a stalking horse in many quarters and simply wouldn't run. By this time John and I had ventured into the deeper recesses of the garden and, to be honest, we were far more interested in its restoration than in having the distraction of animals close by. We mollified Rob by suggesting that we should restore the garden first and then review the situation. The second issue concerned the rallying of our supporters. We decided not only to mount a petition of those in favour, but also to compose a letter of support to the planning officer. This would be photocopied and given to potential supporters with a stamped addressed envelope, leaving them only to mail it with their own signature at the bottom.

John raised a dozen volunteers to doorstep every house in the three parishes whose boundaries dissected the Heligan estate: St Ewe, Mevagissey and Gorran. They were briefed on the detail of the project. For three weeks they canvassed people's homes every evening. Our revised planning application would arrive accompanied by what would turn out to be the first of hundreds of letters of support.

One Saturday night I was woken by the ringing of the telephone and, stirring, I looked at my watch. It was 3 a.m. Your heart races when the phone rings at that time, your mind running riot with thoughts of family tragedy. I snatched up the phone.

In the silence I heard a husky breathing. 'Who is it?' More heavy breathing was followed by a dull click as the receiver was replaced. I returned to bed wondering whether there was a fault on the line. Ten minutes later it rang again and the same thing happened. Four more times it rang before my patience ran out and I took the receiver off the hook.

The next night the same thing happened. On about the third call a voice spoke – a female voice. 'I hate you and I'm watching you,' it said. I was unnerved.

'Who are you? Why are you doing this?' Click.

Week after week the voice came on. We couldn't leave the phone off the hook for fear of missing a real emergency and we couldn't lie there and listen to it ringing. It had become a tyranny and in desperation I called a friend of mine, a private detective, who wired up our phone to catch the voice on tape and get it recognized. Both BT and the police seemed powerless to help. It is an extremely chilling feeling to be watched with hatred by an unknown person. Until it happened to me I would not have believed quite how frightening it could be.

Many bodged attempts later – the slickness of TV doesn't prepare you for the clumsiness of real life when, half asleep, you knock over the machine or put it into fast forward instead of record – we got her on tape. It was 4 a.m. and the phone hadn't rung all night. You don't sleep because you're waiting for it; solving the mystery has become more important than sleeping. You pretend to yourself that it doesn't matter, yet all the time your mind is running an identity parade of potential villains. Suddenly, it rings. Don't move too fast or you'll give her the satisfaction of knowing that she's got through to you – that you're rattled. Pick up the phone with cool deliberation, even though your palms are so sweaty you can hardly hold the receiver. She ranted all the usual stuff, followed by something extraordinary: '*Gehen sie zurück nach Deutschland. Heraus, heraus, heraus, Schweinhund.*'

I recorded it all. Whoever she was, the woman obviously believed that I was German. I am in fact half-Dutch. The comic-style German made the whole thing seem less serious. The fact that someone didn't know my nationality implied that they didn't know much at all.

The strangest thing happened. Two nights later, I was out on the stump collecting signatures. I must have been going for a couple of hours, talking to people and explaining the Heligan plans to them, when I knocked on the door of a house that appeared to be empty. There were no lights on anywhere. I waited for a minute to see if anyone would come and I was just turning to go when the door opened. It was a woman in her late fifties. Her face was the colour of parchment. She peered at me and asked distractedly what I wanted. I recognized the voice instantly and said, 'You? Why?' Her eyes met mine in a brief flicker of recognition, then she turned and slammed the door, refusing to answer my repeated knocking. I left.

The certainty that I now knew who my tormentor was brought total relief. I have neither seen nor heard from her since, though months later I found out her name and what may have driven her to this extraordinary behaviour. It was a tragic story of lost love and dashed hopes associated with Heligan, dating from long before my coming. I just happened to arrive on the scene at the wrong moment.

The next round of the planning battle began in October 1990. It started with an invitation to meet the planning officer, with the local councillors in attendance, to present our new application. This time there was no mention of a rare breeds farm. Brenda Horton, the planning officer's secretary, remarked as I left that never in her life had she seen so many letters in support of anything.

With the planning application lodged it was now a matter of securing the support of the parish councils, whose opinions weigh heavily in the planning process. We navigated safely through the Gorran Parish Council meeting. The first speaker, a local farmer, came out strongly in favour of our plans, and all the other speakers followed his lead. The voting was unanimous.

The St Ewe Parish Council meeting was likely to be more contentious as several protestors were expected to attend. However, I had a stroke of luck when a bat flew into the meeting and, amazingly, I caught it in my hand. I showed it to everyone, recognizing it as a pipistrelle, the smallest of the British bats. At this, my environmental credibility rating went through the roof. They were visibly impressed and luckily didn't ask me if I could recognize any other bats, which would have been tricky. After making my presentation I was asked to leave while they discussed the matter in private. I wandered down to the Crown Inn and found myself at the bar with the leader of the protesters. We talked politely, and soon afterwards the parish councillors trooped in for a drink and announced that we had their total support. The protester was charming and shook my hand and bought me a drink.

At the same time one of the councillors was trying to sell me life insurance.

Mevagissey was always a potential thorn in our side. The council chairman had taken against us and at the Parish Council meeting one councillor after another criticized us, ironically not for what we were intending to do but for what we might do. They rejected our proposal out of hand and I can remember never having felt angrier in my entire life.

As we entered the final furlong, I began meeting the councillors on the Planning Committee in private to canvass support. All of them bar the Mevagissey councillor were now prepared to help, although there were still plenty of passionate protesters convinced that we were going to desecrate the countryside. When John Nelson, Candy and I travelled to the Borough Council Chamber on the afternoon of November 20, the result was far from certain.

We waited for hours for our application to come up. The protesters had gathered in the public gallery and we all tried extremely hard not to look at each other. Our number was called and the Mevagissey councillor was invited to open the batting. He stood up, puffed out his chest, damned us with every word and recommended refusal. The protesters rejoiced and were asked to be silent. We hardly dared breathe. The next contribution was going to be life or death to the project.

Heligan will always have a debt to Councillor Donald Cross. An ex-lawyer and former leader of the council, he stood up and paused for a moment; then he launched into one of the most savage attacks I have ever witnessed from a politician. He demanded to know why the councillor for Mevagissey believed his job was always to protect some unspecified future at the expense of the present, when Heligan had, as we all agreed, potentially one of the finest gardens in Britain – and the alternative was its total loss. There was a murmur in the hall, and one by one the other councillors got up and followed Donald Cross's example. We stormed the vote 11–4. Punching the air, we rushed out of the chamber and dived into the nearest phone box to spread the news, telling everyone to be at the Llawnroc Hotel in an hour's time. Suddenly we were everyone's blue-eyed boys and the bar didn't shut that night. It's funny, but I recall how that evening we drank fit to drown and still we stayed sober. Maybe it was dawning on us that the talking had stopped and we now had to deliver the goods.

This postcard from the 1890s (top) suggests that Heligan's exotic plant collection, drawn from the far corners of the globe, was already a source of pleasure and of pride. A century later, after his earliest expeditions into the undergrowth, John Nelson set about salvaging a glorious past; here (right) with Roger Noyce, cleaning ancient tree ferns in New Zealand.

Our explorations led us into the heart of Heligan where we came upon the old walled gardens, derelict glasshouses and working buildings. Mostly gutted, their timbers rotten, these ruins had an all-pervading sadness that captivated the imagination ...

... the finial of a glasshouse gable-end at a crazy angle, like a sinking ship.

In time the earth would yield up its treasures too ... a large collection of plant labels bore the marks of those who created the gardens ... while, exposed to daylight again, the old Britannia boiler wore a mournful expression.

Heligan House in the 1880s lay at the heart of a thriving estate.

An aerial picture from the 1950s shows Heligan House with the Home Farm
buildings and the glasshouses of the Flower Garden behind. With its large staff
no more than a distant memory, the estate was in decline.

The Italian Garden, inspired by John Claude 'Jack' Tremayne's love affair with Italy, had been the final creation – here being admired by visitors during the 1920s.

Jack Tremayne (top) relaxes in the summerhouse of his new 'Suntrap' or Italian Garden, built in 1909. By 1990, its once formal laurel hedge and original kiwi fruit had grown rampant, completely concealing all trace of his design and only after clearance the following year were its bare bones revealed.

Breathing life back into the Italian Garden was our first big project and the original kiwi fruit soon flourished again among its new neighbours.

Derelict vinery

Bee-bole lawn

Main drive to Heligan House

Ravine

Italian Garden

Vegetable Garden

Flora's Green

Palm Cottage

Flower Garden

Melon Garden

Northern Summerhouse

Sundial Garden

Derelict peach house

New Zealand

The view from the summerhouse in the Italian Garden (opposite) echoes that captured in the earlier archival shot. In 1992 this restored pool could be seen clearly from the air, as well as our re-seeded 'Flora's Brown' and the still derelict and overgrown productive areas of the Northern Gardens.

The Lost Gardens of Heligan were officially opened to the public on Good Friday, April 17, 1992. The occasion was very much a family affair. A towering rhododendron (opposite) stands sentinel at the new visitor entrance to the Northern Gardens.

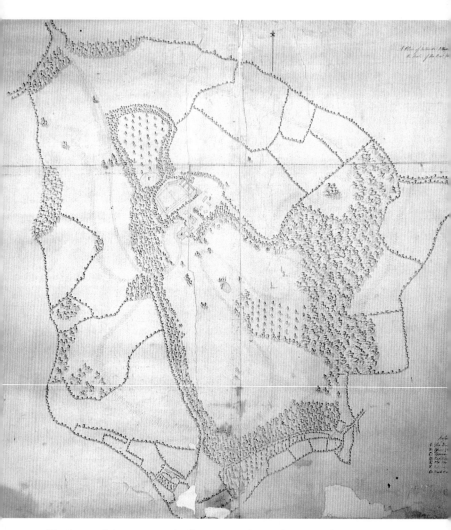

The Cornwall County Record Office contained more than 3,000 documents relating to Heligan, many of which had already been carefully researched and logged by Ivor Herring, a local historian. Among these papers were a number of plans for the gardens and the wider estate which proved invaluable references as we tried to re-establish order out of the chaos on the ground. This plan of 'Intended alterations for Hilligan [*sic*] the seate of the Rev. Mr Tremayne', pre-1810, signed 'Thos. Gray', is perhaps the most important. The main shape of the Northern Gardens is set by a tree-lined circular ride which runs within the boundary walls of the parkland. This is the area that will become Flora's Green and the Vegetable Garden, but is here still shown as orchard. Below this, one can clearly make out the shape of the Melon Garden (at least the rear wall of it and some pits inside) and the Flower Garden, as well as the earlier pair of small walled gardens which today abut its eastern wall. The whole is surrounded by an impressive shelter belt of trees that would offer protection from the prevailing south-westerly winds for the gardens that would be developed within.

Chapter 3

THE SECRET OF THE
THUNDERBOX ROOM

The great doors hung, half-open, from their rusty hinges.
The sun-bleached paint, brittle and peeling so that here
and there the wood showed through rough and weathered,
had lost its colour long ago. Only in the recesses where the
sun never shone could traces of the original dark green be
seen. Layer upon layer, the paint symbolized the rigour of
the head gardener's maintenance regime. These doors were
once barred by a slip bolt of four-by-one timber, leaving as
the only point of entry a small service wicket within the one
on the right-hand side. Above the entrance, a lintel of oak
balanced precariously, the stonework it supported loosened
by the roots of an ash tree that had set itself on the parapet
many years before.

We had cut our way through dense clumps of invasive
bamboo, drawn towards a perfectly formed palm that stood
sentinel at the entrance to what was obviously a walled garden. John Nelson and I were on another of our explorations,
venturing deeper into the gardens each time. Today we were
excited; somehow we knew it was going to be a special day.
You can feel these things.

Once inside, we paused for a moment. There was a sense

that we were trespassing, that we had come upon a secret shrine. In the gloaming we could see dozens of trees growing thickly together, woven into a solid mass by an extremely vigorous climbing plant that covered everything like a furry blanket. We had never seen anything like this before. Under the trees we could make out shapes at once familiar and other-worldly. This was clearly the area of the garden where the real work had taken place. There were three long frame-bases of decreasing sizes. Against the back wall of the largest of them we found a collection of windows stacked as if for future use, their dimensions suggesting that they were the original lights for the frames. They were totally rotten, but held in place by their own weight, and remarkably the glass was still intact. This was cut in a distinctive style, scalloped on its leading edge and of varying sizes, as if glass had been too precious to waste in the name of uniformity.

Close by, we could make out the rear wall of what had once been a greenhouse. The stone quoins which had supported the main load-carrying beam now cantilevered out into open space, breaching the curtain of ivy and bramble which smothered the rest of the structure. Its main timbers had fallen in years ago, with only the eastern doorway, and the windows that abutted it, left standing to give any indication of its original form. Outside the door a pair of substantial chimney-pots stood side by side, again giving the impression that someone was about to make use of them.

As we worked our way further around we came upon other structures built against the walls. They had spaces for windows and the roofs had fallen in, and as we broke into the first building we became aware of the crunching of slates under our feet. We hugged the walls gingerly. John and I had put the wind up each other a little by discussing the possibility of falling down a hidden well. No one would ever find us here, and the thought of adding to Heligan's mysteries by spending our last moments thrashing about in black water was enough to bring us out in goosebumps.

An enormous moss-covered trough with a brass tap at one end had played host, many moons ago, to two sycamore saplings that had rooted between it and the wall. The trees were now mature and the wall behind was bowing under the pressure. The downpipe which once fed the trough had now become woven into the living architecture. There were ferns everywhere, covering the ground, the walls and even nestling in the branches of the trees where they competed for a home with a startling array of lichens.

A single granite upright loomed out of some laurels that had taken possession of the south-western corner of the yard. The lime markings on the wall behind showed the line of the roof it had once supported. Nearby we found another granite, prostrate and partly buried by slates. It was only when we had ducked under a large horse chestnut growing out of the middle frame that we saw the walls of a two-storey building, resembling a little cottage, now gutted and open to the sky. Its windows remained eerily in place, framed by the ivy which had rooted in the wall plate above. A single roof truss hung crazily in mid-air, held in position by the overgrowth. The upstairs room was plastered and yet the ground floor, which was full almost to ceiling height with rubble, was not. The floor joists had rotted out long ago, and some of them lay balanced against the wall where they had snapped off. Their ends were rotted from too many seasons of Cornish rain, and held in position by the red tiles that had once roofed the building. John warned me to be careful – the whole front wall of the building rocked when you leant against it. He saw something in one of the joist holes and chuckled. 'It's been a long time since a chicken was encouraged to lay with one of these,' he said, pulling out a perfect ceramic egg. He presumed a rat had found it and had taken it off, only to be hugely disappointed.

We moved on, cutting the velvety limbs of the mysterious climber as we went. The building was in two unequal parts, with a dividing wall two thirds of the way along. Here we came upon a doorway with a lintel so low that one couldn't imagine people comfortably walking through. Our speculations about the bonsai stature of the Victorians were abruptly terminated when John knocked on the lintel and it fell apart, causing the adjacent wall to creak ominously. Through the doorway we could just make out the top of a set of granite steps that led straight into the back wall. This was plastered, but weathering had revealed cracks in the unmistakable shape of a doorway. The steps, we supposed, had probably serviced further working buildings on the other side of the wall, whose purpose we could only guess at. There might even have been an exotic fruit house, making the best of the south-facing wall. Presumably, once these had fallen from use, the entrance had been blocked off. It was hard to control our curiosity. We considered clambering up the wall to take a peek over the top, but its condition was so dangerous that we resisted the temptation. We would save that adventure for another day.

This part of the two-storey building was set into the north-western corner of the frame yard. The velvet climber was holding up a small part of the roof and there were joists and boards still in place at floor level. Though the roof tiles swayed precariously every time we moved, we couldn't contain our urge to poke around inside the two little ground-floor rooms. The rubble was less deep here in the shelter of the floor above, and John and I began to pull debris out by hand. John rooted around until he found the slate floor. He sat down on the pile he had just made and lit a match for a better look. 'Bloody hell,' he said, laughing. 'I know what this place was for. It's a thunderbox room, you know, a khazi.' He pointed out the cement fillet which had held the wooden seat in place, and there was no argument, the proportions made it obvious. 'And this is the bucket,' he said, waving a rusty object around his head. 'They didn't waste good manure in those days, you know. It probably went straight on the garden.' The answer to my inevitable question about toilet paper was either moss or dock leaves.

My attention had been caught by something on the wall. John lit another match and I crawled over for a closer look. It was graffiti. There in the plaster, unmistakably, you could make out writing. I nudged John in the ribs and we got close up to the wall and lit another match. We were in high good spirits and fully prepared for some of the ribaldry normally associated with toilet graffiti. To our amazement we were faced with a rather sombre one-liner. Though the heavy pencil had faded over the years one could still clearly read:

'Don't come here to sleep or to slumber.'

Underneath were the signatures of those who had sat in this place, which was so cramped and dark that it wouldn't have given much encouragement to do either: W. Durnsford, W. Guy, R. Barron, C. Dyer, C. Ball, Albert Rowe, W. Rose, three Paynters (initials illegible), Vercoe, Vickery, L. Warne, D. Hocking, Carhart ... there were more, but we couldn't read them.

A simple love-heart, almost obscured by mould, bore the names David and Charlotte. It seemed an inauspicious place to advertise your love, unless of course it was a piece of mischief. In even fainter pencil we found a date: August 1914. At the time this was being written, events in the Balkans (somewhere few of them would have heard of, still less cared about) were conspiring to destroy the world as they knew it. I remembered reading somewhere that the summer of 1914 had been exceptionally hot. It is easy to imagine the optimism of the time – and feel a pit in your stomach when you realize what was in store for them: the muddy fields of Flanders, the distant killing grounds of Gallipoli and Palestine. It was the end of their confident expectation of the uninterrupted ebb and flow of life. Only later would we begin to understand its impact on this small community.

We had been more moved than either of us might have anticipated by the writing on the wall. It had brought the garden alive for us. Real people had led real lives here, and we now knew some of their names. It felt at once like a shared intimacy and an invasion of privacy. We could not ignore it even if we wanted to.

There are many good reasons one could have for wanting to restore a garden; each one has a story to tell and special pleasures to enjoy. However, John and I decided that day that preserving Heligan for posterity by putting it in aspic was not what we wanted. We had flesh and blood in mind. We wanted to hold a mirror up to the past and tell the story of these people, in a way we hoped they would have understood and approved of. Just as importantly, we wanted to celebrate the lives of all those ordinary men and women who had once worked in great gardens like these. It would be a completely new way of telling an old story, yet still relevant to so many whose forefathers had toiled in such places. More than anything, the desire to capture the essential spirit of place became the raison d'être of the restoration. I felt instantly that there was a story to tell here that would move people.

Soon afterwards I was waiting for friends to join me at the

Crown at St Ewe, and to kill time I crossed the road to the graveyard. St Ewe is the perfect country church. A palm tree and a large camellia hug the path to the doorway, giving the place an exotic feel. The camellia takes its name – 'St Ewe' – from the village, and was bred locally on the Williamses' magnificent Caerhays Castle estate, a place of pilgrimage for plantsmen since the turn of the century. The camellia's waxy, deep green leaves and pink flowers frame a simple granite war memorial.

The grey drizzly day reflected my mood as I took in the view across the graveyard, over lichen-covered gravestones and memorials packed tight inside its boundary walls. Save for the occasional simple posy of remembrance to the more recently departed the graves were mostly untended, yet there was a curious, bustling vitality to the scene. The Gothick atmosphere brought to mind lines from Gray's wonderful poem 'Elegy, Written in a Country Churchyard':

Beneath those rugged elms, that yew tree's shade
  Where heaves the turf in many a mouldering heap
Each in his narrow cell for ever laid,
  The rude forefathers of the hamlet sleep . . .

Some village Hampden, that with dauntless breast
  The little tyrant of his fields withstood,
Some mute inglorious Milton here may rest,
  Some Cromwell, guiltless of his country's blood . . .

Far from the madding crowd's ignoble strife,
  Their sober wishes never learn'd to stray;
Along the cool sequester'd vale of life
  They kept the noiseless tenor of their way.

Yet e'en these bones from insult to protect
  Some frail memorial still erected nigh
With uncouth rhymes and shapeless sculpture deck'd,
  Implores the passing tribute of a sigh.

Gray's timeless lines celebrate the virtues and the often unrealized potential of men and women whose coming and passing remain largely unremarked, except in St Ewe and thousands of communities like it. On the other hand, as De Gaulle's wry comment had it, the graveyards of the world are full of irreplaceable men.

I decided to explore the church itself. A bank of brass light-switches fell to hand inside the door and soon the church was ablaze with light. The simplicity of its stone and timber construction felt absolutely right; the choir screen, with its intricately carved latticework, is the only sign of ornamentation in the formal sense, though the barrel-vaulted roof, with its strong and impressively jointed members in the Gothic style, is of great beauty.

This was the church of the Tremaynes, the creators of Heligan. Most were christened here, some were married and almost all were laid to rest. In the intervening times they contributed to its partial rebuilding, dedicated memorial stained-glass windows, and donated flowers and produce for services and special occasions. Their family vault was here. In the middle of the southernmost aisle lay a large slate with a recessed handle. Its edges fitted under the adjacent pews, so that they needed to be moved at such time as a body was to be interred. Curiously, at first glance the slate seemed to bear the arms of the Isle of Man. Closer inspection revealed three arms rampant, joined in a circle. This affected Frenchification, de rigueur in the eighteenth century, was meant to signify Tremayne, *trois mains*, three hands. The motif appears elsewhere in the church, both in the stained-glass windows and on the large diamond-shaped picture bearing the complete range of arms associated with the family, which sits above the southern door. It is set in a gilt frame with a border of linked thigh bones, an hourglass and a skull, an unnervingly secular collection of images.

Once outside I decided for no particular reason to take a closer look at the war memorial. The few names were well spaced on three sides of the cross, in alphabetical order with initials, surname and village of origin etched in brass. C.E. Ball of Polsue, P. Carhart of Pengrugla, D. Hocking of St Ewe, L. Warne of Trelewack: these names were horribly familiar – I'd been introduced to them only days before. Our bitter-sweet musings on lost innocence now seemed dangerously sentimental. The truth was nasty, vivid and full of pain, and only the passing of seventy years or more would dull it back to sepia.

I decided to visit the other war memorials in the neighbouring parishes to see if there were any other familiar names. In due course the Mevagissey stone was to give up R. Barron and C. Dyer. The Gorran Church memorial revealed the names of William Guy, who died in France on April 13, 1918 while serving with the Duke of Cornwall's Light Infantry, and Charles Ball of the 10th Worcestershires, also killed in France ten days earlier.

To say that the First World War was catastrophic for Heligan is to overstate the case, but not by much. The loss of manpower and the resulting austerity began a decline from which it was never going to recover. My mind was drawn back to the strange feeling we'd had on our first visit to what we now know as the Melon Garden. It sounds odd, but we had the impression that everyone had left the garden in the middle of a working day, fully intending to come back. For seventy years Heligan had waited, with the garden in mourning like a naval widow forever looking out to sea for a husband who never returns.

Chapter 4

THE ROAD FROM GORRAN TO DAMASCUS

Our discoveries in the Melon Garden inspired John and me with a clear purpose for the restoration of the lost gardens. And now that we had planning permission to open the gardens to the public we needed a strategy to realize our dream. Fortune smiled on us in the form of the man who had recently restored Trebah Gardens near Mawnan Smith.

Major Tony Hibbert MC is one of the most singular men I have ever had the good luck to meet. He had bought Trebah on his retirement, so that he and his wife Eira could sip gin and tonics looking into the sunset and maybe do some sailing. He knew little or nothing about gardening and was astonished to discover that the overgrown mess in the valley below his house had once been a fine and celebrated planted landscape. It had been designed in the nineteenth century by the Fox family, renowned gardeners who had created a series of superb valley gardens along the Helford River. Tony got stuck in and in his seventies was using chain-saws, climbing trees and picking up the garden lingo as if born to it. Trebah is magnificent and looks as if it would be more at home in Hawaii than in Britain. Tony had first tried to donate it to the National Trust, which had turned it down on the grounds that the endowment wasn't big enough. This forced him to look at ways of opening the gardens to the public himself and making them pay their own way. He was, on his own admission, much influenced by the words of the Duke of Bedford, who wrote a book about his experiences at Woburn. This book refers to the three most important aspects of a garden that is to be opened to the public: one, the car park must have shade for the dogs left in cars, because the British are dog lovers; two, good loos are vital as visitors judge you on your loos, not your garden; three, the tearooms must be first class. The gardens themselves don't really feature at all. Tony took the advice to heart and built up a hugely successful enterprise which out-performed all its rivals, bringing visitors to Cornwall from all over the country and abroad.

It was Tony who had, in 1988, started the Cornwall Gardens Trust and encouraged the registration and survey of the existing gardens in the county, with a view to evaluating their importance and, if at all possible, securing their futures. Heligan had been appraised during his stint as chairman and, as he now readily admits (in the preface to the Heligan guide book), he had consigned it to his bin of lost causes.

However, he was an inspiration to us, and genuinely enthusiastic about Heligan's potential. He gave me a tour of his garden, a lecture on the Duke of Bedford with a copy of the book to take with me, a budget showing how Trebah performed – and a promise that he would come to see me soon to help me sort out a few practical matters. Tony had won his MC at the Battle of Arnhem, so when he discovered that I was a Dutchman and that my family came from Arnhem he was delighted. He has two ornamental ponds at

Trebah named after his two Dutch god-daughters, the children of the Dutch resistance leader who helped him to escape after the battle.

The lease was taking a long time to extract from the estate, which seemed set on labyrinthine negotiations with our lawyers. In common with everyone else we met, they were working in the hope of jam tomorrow. My job was to secure the jam. We had by now spoken to many of the potential grant-giving bodies, including the Rural Development Commission (RDC), the Countryside Commission and English Heritage. The key problem was that before any of them could award a grant, they had to know how much the work was going to cost. No one we knew had undertaken a restoration on anything like this scale, so there was no way of knowing how we ought to price it. As a first step, John invited numerous contractors to put a figure on particular aspects of the restoration, the idea being that the completed jigsaw of quotations would act as the basis for any grant application. They duly came and looked around but all, bar one, backed off. Underpricing could be ruinous and there was no basis on which to bid.

We were getting desperate. Something was needed to break the gridlock.

Salvation came in the shape of Nigel Mathews, the Cornwall County Council landscape architect, whose job it was to allocate small grants for the protection or restoration of the local heritage. I took him round the garden and made a plea for help. When the award for £1000 came through the post we were beside ourselves with relief. John Nelson could now clear one acre of overgrowth and give us a benchmark for pricing the whole job.

At the end of January 1991 John came into his own. Now

was the time for action. Alongside him on Day One was a digger driver, a chainsaw operator and his own brother-in-law. Chainsaws blazed, diggers dug, machetes slashed and a mountainous fire turned an acre of debris into no more than a small pile of ash. Our first area of cleared ground felt like an encampment, a safe haven. John was like a man possessed. Despite running two other building jobs simultaneously, he came to Heligan every afternoon and put in four or five hours' work. After the first fortnight of bulk clearance, he was joined by Dave Burns, the merchant seaman who had helped rescue my chimney after the hurricane. From the first moment he clapped eyes on the place he threw in his lot with us and worked all his shore leave in the gardens, for the sheer love of it.

Just before Christmas my sister Vicky had come to stay, putting her typewriter and secretarial skills at my service. We spent four long days assembling a proposal to interest television companies: *The Secret Garden* and *Peter Rabbit* meet *Challenge Anneka*, we thought. To keep up the project's momentum we would need to bring in sponsors, and there is no better way of attracting sponsors than with the promise of exposure on prime-time television. Once completed, the proposal was sent to *Gardeners' World*, then at BBC Pebble Mill, and to the local ITV company, TSW.

The response was immediate. First out of the stalls were *Gardeners' World*, who phoned up asking hundreds of further questions about the project. Stephanie Silk, the producer, said that she would call back over the next few days to arrange a site visit. Immediately thereafter we were called by TSW, who were just as enthusiastic and insisted that one of their directors should come and see us the following day. Mr TSW turned up dressed for the Oscars rather than for a three-mile hike through some of the most uncompromising vegetation in Britain. He wore a cashmere suit, a splendid pair of patent leather shoes and had a wife who was apparently extremely interested in gardening. His own gardening was, he admitted, done from the comfort of a chair in the company of a Scotch.

The day was only about a hundred metres old when the cashmere suit started to fray under close scrutiny from the brambles. Trying to distract him, I held out the temptation of being the first person to explore the once famed sub-tropical valley garden to the south of Heligan House. He seemed genuinely keen on the prospect so we veered off, rounded the house and dived into the undergrowth. Hundreds of sycamores and ash trees had obliterated the shape of the landscape so totally that it was difficult to get our bearings. There were no obvious paths and the famous lakes seemed to have disappeared.

The only indication that this had once been a garden was the large number of bamboos and tropical-looking tree ferns that were growing in magnificent clumps despite the shade of the trees. I was concentrating hard on keeping my balance when I heard a low moan behind me. Mr TSW was slowly sinking up to his waist in stagnant mud, hidden under the cover of the leaves. In hindsight it was impolite of me to get so excited about the discovery of the lake and perhaps I should have been more sympathetic about the loss of his shoe. All hope of a documentary with TSW sank with him, a fact confirmed later that evening with a terse fax which even forgot to thank me for the glorious day we'd had.

Stephanie Silk was something else altogether. Highly pro-fessional, tough and chic, she approached us like a sapper in a minefield. Question after question came pouring out of my fax, until she relented and set a date for her arrival. She was clearly captivated from the first moment she saw Heligan, but kept a distance because she was worried that however magnificent and romantic it looked in the flesh, its attraction would be difficult to capture on the small screen. She was also concerned that any film would have to show the 'before and after', and on such a scale that there was a danger we could be left with pictures of one of the world's biggest building sites. Later, over dinner, she broached the subject with John, who, without batting an eyelid, informed her that he fully expected to have completed the restoration within twelve months. By the end of the evening he had convinced me, let alone Stephanie Silk.

The following morning we rose full of remorse. Had we been a little ambitious with the truth? And if we had, should we say so? I knew that without the commitment of a TV company we would find it difficult to make things happen. Once committed, they would have to work to make it successful – so we decided that the interests of the garden came first and remained silent. Stephanie left promising a draft shooting script within the fortnight and we knew that she had taken the bait. Although there were a couple of hiccups along the way, the contract which arrived in early February gave me, at long last, the armoury I needed to go out into the world and raise the money to get on with the project.

Two important issues needed resolving immediately: the protection of, and access to, all areas of the garden. These essentials could only be achieved through the co-operation of the neighbouring tenant farmers, John Clark and John Nancarrow. They kindly agreed to give up the strips of land we needed, to enable us to put in a network of linking paths and to plant new shelter belts. The recent hurricane had shown the West Country estates just how vulnerable they were to extreme weather.

The hereditary aristocracy may be a difficult institution to defend in an era in which the development of a meritocracy is held up as being politically desirable, but there is no better system for the encouragement of long-term investment in the land and the social infrastructure needed to maintain it. The awareness of a duty to plan for future generations goes hand in hand with the knowledge that present enjoyment is based on foundations laid in the past. A stake in the land demands the long-term view, in a way that would be impossible for us ordinary people. Many of the great gardens of England were developed within secure micro-climates created by the prescient shelter belt plantings of previous generations. Economic constraints, but more often simple complacency after the First World War, led to a widespread neglect of the values of good husbandry, which rendered many of the by now over-mature gardens vulnerable to natural disaster. The extreme hurricane damage in the South East of England in 1987 and the South West in 1990 was in many cases the result of events deep in the past. Had regular planting schemes been in place, with older trees being removed when past their prime and new ones brought on, the storms would have had much less impact.

At Heligan, now that there were huge gaps throughout the shelter belt, the threat was potentially disastrous. The force of the wind was being funnelled into vulnerable areas. The re-planting of the shelter belts had to be our primary concern.

Ironically, but for the hurricane, Heligan would probably have been lost for ever, a footnote in a learned journal the only reminder of its existence. In 1987, with the South East so ravaged that many of its great gardens had been brought to the brink of extinction, the Countryside Commission was forced to act. The Government put money aside for an initiative named Task Force Trees. Initially it was restricted to granting assistance for clearing-up operations in the aftermath of the storms, but soon a wider interpretation, encompassing restoration work, fell into place. So when the 1990 hurricane hit the South West, the instruments were ready to cope and all that was needed was a widening of the geographical area covered by the scheme. By Christmas 1990, Heligan was almost eligible for storm damage assistance – but not quite.

Heligan House was a Grade II listed building on the English Heritage Register, and although this designation covered the house and the walls of the walled gardens, with a grey area concerning the land contained within them, it did not cover the garden as a whole. The Countryside Commission was legally able to assist only gardens that had been listed in their own right. The gardens of Heligan were unlisted, not least because they were impenetrable and there-fore unvisited when the register was drawn up. The Countryside Commission was sympathetic to our case for listing and put me in touch with English Heritage, to whom I explained our predicament. Soon an independent assessor came to see us. Despite only being able to gain access to some of the garden, she felt able to award it an interim Grade II status. We were in business.

The blanks were filled in a little more when we discovered that the last head gardener at Heligan was still alive and living in Mevagissey. A few enquiries later and I was having tea with Fred Varcoe, a former employee of the Thomas family who had rented Heligan from the Tremayne Estate after the Second World War. Fred hadn't been back to the gardens for nearly thirty years, because it made him so sad to see the decay. He reminisced about the Thomases, of whom he was very fond, and startled me by saying that Mrs Pat Thomas was still alive and that her daughter Sue worked locally as a personal assistant at the headquarters of the National Trust at Lanhydrock. Indeed, he had seen them only recently and had been shown many slides taken in the gardens by the late Commander Thomas. He believed their collection also contained photographs which had been found in the house and predated the Thomases' stay there.

He brought out some of Commander Thomas's hand-written planting notes for the camellias and rhododendrons on the main rides of the Northern Gardens at Heligan, which he let me take away for copying. Then he showed me a photograph of the house, covered in ivy. The ladies were all in gingham dresses and the men in tails. Fred thought he remembered being told that the occasion was a party to welcome George V on his tour to Cornwall. He went on to explain that part of his responsibility had been to operate the hydraulic ram pumps in the valley to the south of the house. They had pumped water more than a mile up to a large reservoir on what is now Pengrugla campsite. On a still night the low thump of the rams had been quite eerie, as if the earth had a heartbeat, and the noise had carried right down the valley to Mevagissey. As he warmed to his subject he told me of the great tree which was supposed to be half oak and half beech. It grew near Flora's Green, the lawn at the northern end of the garden, and was rumoured to have been specially created by a renowned arboriculturist to the Danish Court to celebrate the wedding of Princess Alexandra and the future Edward VII in 1863. Fred was sure that it must still be there.

I asked him what the gardens had been like when he had arrived after the Second World War and he confirmed that they were in a similar state to how we had recently found them. A decision was taken to maintain the still accessible main rides and walks to the east and west which led up to Flora's Green. This was completely surrounded by beautiful rhododendrons. The Thomases had worked very hard, and even after Commander Thomas died they bred hydrangeas and camellias for the cut flower market at Covent Garden. He remembered fondly that they had kept up the tradition of supplying St Ewe Church with cut flowers for services and special occasions.

I left with Mrs Thomas's phone number. She was delighted that someone was taking an interest in Heligan and confirmed that she had some photographs which she would be happy to lend me. I felt as if we were making a start on the jigsaw puzzle.

I now needed to concentrate on finding the horticultural expertise to carry out the restoration. An extremely convoluted set of coincidences led to the tracking down, through a former pupil, of Alan Mitchell. Probably the country's leading dendrologist, he was the author of some of the seminal works on British and European trees. It was Alan's tree surveys carried out at Heligan in 1959 and again in 1975 which formed the basis of our knowledge of the fine specimens we had in the garden. Ivor Herring had let us have copies of these, and we had shown them to the Silvanus Woodland Trust, who had agreed to update them for us. When we discovered that Alan was still alive and, what's more, prepared to return to Heligan, Silvanus, far from being put out, became hugely excited at the prospect. He was their guru and they felt privileged to walk with him. I met him only once, on the one visit he made in 1991, but his piercing eyes, good humour and gentleness with those who hung on his every word made it a special occasion. He was reputedly the oldest card-carrying Communist in England, and his habit of walking in open-toed sandals in all weathers made him a legend. He was rumoured to be the only man alive who could differentiate the several hundred varieties of oak to be found in the UK. Tree after tree he would touch like an old friend, commenting on where he had seen other fine examples of the species. Though suffering from acute angina and diabetes, he became so enthusiastic that he only realized that he hadn't eaten for six hours when he started to suffer a diabetic attack four miles deep into the woods. Sue Pring had to lead him out for his own good.

A little before this I had heard on the grapevine that Cornwall had appointed a new county horticultural adviser, the former director of RHS Wisley, Philip McMillan Browse. He was to be based at the county demonstration garden at Probus, not far from Heligan. Part of his brief was to give advice to garden owners and horticulturists around the county and he readily accepted an invitation to come and see us. From the moment he arrived it was obvious that he was the man we needed. At the same time it was just as obvious that at this stage in the restoration we could not afford someone of this quality. His confidence and sureness of touch were inspiring. The importance of his position might have made him aloof but, on the contrary, he was as enthusiastic as we were. His past as director of Wisley and, before that, of the Saratoga Institute in California had given him a broad knowledge of the world of horticulture, and his roots as a native of the Isles of Scilly made him sympathetic to the project. Perhaps he felt a sense of homecoming; but also, I think, the derelict productive gardens reminded him of a simpler horticulture – the growing of things for the table – which had inspired him to enter the field in the first place.

Philip reassured us that we didn't need a head gardener at this stage, and that he could supervise the work of the volunteers. We were even more delighted when he offered to take responsibility for all horticultural matters at Heligan with immediate effect. When, soon afterwards, I hosted a visit by Peter Borlase, the head gardener to the National Trust at Lanhydrock, Philip was even more bullish, assuring me that Heligan could be one of the most important gardens in Britain.

Around this time we also came across the British Trust for Conservation Volunteers (BTCV), a voluntary organization dedicated to teaching countryside management skills and team leadership, through a mixture of formal courses and informal working holidays, open to all. These groups, of up to twelve people at a time, can be a remarkable cocktail of ages, backgrounds and professional achievements. All most volunteers have in common is a desire to do something at once social, out of doors and out of the ordinary. What they look for are challenging projects with a specific goal.

Our first meeting was with a marvellous man in his early sixties called George Crumpler. He was a team leader and part of his job was to recce potential projects, before deciding whether or not they should be included on the BTCV list of holidays. After filming everything with his camcorder and explaining the procedure, he said that he would be recommending Heligan, and before you could say machete we had a working weekend booked up for March. George even brought in a specialist chainsaw man; and Rob persuaded an old friend of his, Orlando Rutter, a team leader from the Slapton Ley Field Centre in Devon, to join us as well.

During one of our earliest expeditions to the interior, John Nelson and I had come upon a massive growth of laurel somewhere towards the centre of the garden. The laurels reached fully fifty feet into the air and had formed a massive and impenetrable canopy which entwined on one side with the top branches of an avenue of extremely tall but leggy rhododendrons, and on the other side arched into the middle distance until brought to a halt by a long brick wall. We had crawled under the all-embracing branches to take a look inside. When our eyes had adjusted to the greeny underworld we could dimly make out an iron archway which stood at the centre of what had once been a formal laurel hedge – the entrance to a private garden. We scrabbled around at the base of the archway until we felt the cold iron of an ornamental gate buried in the loam. It had swung here until its rusting hinges could hold the weight no longer and it had fallen among the leaves. A series of steps led up to a plateau where a pedestal of granite stood to attention before us, poking out from under the debris. Next to it, and strangely out of context, lay a cracked and discoloured washing copper. As we cautiously moved forward the ground gave way and we sank through the carpet of leaves into what could have been a small pool. The canopy above us was thinning to a dense but lighter weave of laurel and furry creeper, with a dash of willow coming from a pair that had set their roots nearby. At the far end some terracotta roof tiles lay where they had fallen from their previous home, which now loomed in front of us. Wide steps led up to a small open-fronted rectangular building. Two wobbly brick entrance pillars still stood, but the roof had caved in under the weight of the laurel and creeper.

Peering through the undergrowth, we could see a large rhododendron pinioned to the ground by a fallen oak and a palm tree. We had the impression that it wouldn't be many autumns before all trace of human hand had been erased.

When George asked us to select an achievable weekend's task for his BTCV group, this area, which we now knew from Ivor Herring's notes to be called the Suntrap or Italian Garden, was the obvious choice. To give him a feel for the general layout we repeated the journey we'd made before. He was as excited as we were by the prospect and gave a running commentary to his camcorder filming, in tones worthy of the discovery of Tutankhamun's tomb. When we emerged from the shadows, he got out his notebook and wrote a shopping list of requirements for the project to come. This was the start of a relationship with the BTCV which happily lasts to this day.

Over the year which had passed since my first glimpse of the gardens, Rob Poole and I had been going backwards and forwards between the accountants, the lawyers and the estate. The trip to London was as familiar as the drive to Heligan, but by the end of February 1991 we knew that we had a plausible business plan, and a lease that seemed to be negotiated all bar the shouting. With a first-class horticultural adviser, the benefit of some scholarly research and a TV documentary in the making, we had every reason to feel confident.

March 3, 1991 was the first day of the restoration proper. George Crumpler had met the volunteers from the station the previous evening and had taken them back to St Ewe Village Hall, where they passed an extremely uncomfortable night sleeping on the floor. Next morning the BTCV team turned up on the dot of nine in a Transit van stuffed with tools, picnic materials and waterproofs, and set to work under John and George's careful eye. Chainsaws roared into action and for two days there was a continuous sound of tearing, ripping, crashing and later crackling as the debris was burnt up in a series of bonfires around the site. The laurels were cut right down to stump to encourage them to regrow into a hedge. The furry climber, identified by Philip McMillan Browse as *Actinidia chinensis*, the Chinese gooseberry or kiwi fruit, was carefully cut back so that the clearance could be total. The fallen oak and the palm tree were sawn up so that after two days' work we could see from the arched gateway to the summerhouse. The rubbish had been burned and several tons of timber stacked for future use. All that remained was the huge rhododendron that still lay on its side. John and Orlando banked up its roots with earth. Later they would winch it upright (after it had finished flowering, so that the trauma of its lifting wouldn't kill it). The bank managers, physicist, baker, plumber and students who made up that first BTCV crew all agreed that it was the most exciting holiday they had ever had and many of them vowed to return. They drove off into the sunset with happy memories of having achieved the improbable – and John sat down to work out a campaign for the television company to deliver the impossible.

One evening at the end of March the *Gardeners' World* crew turned up. Stephanie was in overdrive and accompanied by Stefan Buczacki, who would present the programme. We walked the gardens at a military clip, after which she got hold of John and asked him to reveal which area he would restore first. He showed her the Italian Garden.

'Will it be finished in time?' she demanded, worried about her filming schedule.

'Most certainly,' said John.

The restoration would be guided by a ground survey, together with the evidence of a single photograph lent to us by Charity Rowlandson, a senior resident in Heligan House.

(She herself, as a child, had played in these gardens, having come here as a house guest between the wars. Her reliable memory and enthusiasm for the restoration were to serve us well over the next few years.) The view, taken from the summerhouse, was of a family group standing beside the pool, with the archway set in the shadows of a clipped laurel hedge. Judging by their dress it was taken in the early 1920s.

The BTCV clearance had revealed the shape of the garden but it became apparent that all the structures and plantings, save the kiwi fruit, had been lost. Working from the photograph, John and Dave, accompanied by two volunteers, set to. The first task was to remove all the roots and stumps from the pool and the newly discovered 'flower bed' against the wall. The dumper truck was used as a winch to pull out all the protesting stumps and then John marked out the bed and had it dug and dug again until it was completely clean. Next he set out strings to show where the paving should go. The original was so disturbed that he would have to start again, using the same stones. The steps up through the arch were relaid first and then the path around the pool. (The old path had been set in lime and topped with a fillet of earth to encourage the growth of creeping herbs which when crushed underfoot would have released their perfume.) This was followed by the re-rendering of the pool, which didn't have an overflow. This odd omission caused the pool to flood into the gateside flower bed every time there was a heavy downpour – a problem from which we still suffer and one which makes the growing of Mediterranean plants there extremely challenging. To cheer us up one of the volunteers donated a garden gnome which was placed on the pedestal in the middle of the pool, keeping mock guard until one night it was stolen. The gnome's place would eventually be taken by something more elegant.

With the film crew breathing down his neck, John set to work on the summerhouse. The wobbly pillars came down, and then went up again. The new roof timbers were fixed in place. John and I located replacement terracotta roof tiles in Devon and these also went on at the speed of light.

The kiwi bled like a stuck pig. Not the drip-drip-drip you might expect, but a gushing that flowed unabated for six weeks. There were lakes of sticky liquid under every severed limb and we felt very guilty. Philip, an expert on *Actinidia chinensis*, had been excited to realize that this was probably one of the original plants introduced in the early 1900s by Veitch's Nursery in Exeter, grown from seed brought back by 'Chinese' Wilson from Szechuan in China. We thought we'd killed it.

The pool was filled. Philip emptied his home pond of lilies and other assorted water plants. Yuccas were found from Probus and every friend with a cordyline or phormium was persuaded to part with it. Philip went on a mad spree, defying his normally houseproud nature. He filled his car up with various clianthus, euphorbia and melianthus, which were planted out; and at last the large rhododendron, which by this time had finished flowering, was winched upright.

The kiwi was not dead. First it had broken out in red spots like the measles. Then it decided to grow like the clappers. It put on inches every day. In week one we were all excited, thinking it would cover up a piece of wall nicely in time for filming. In week two it wouldn't stop. The wall coverage was good, but we'd got enough. By week three we had a problem. We consulted Philip, who informed us that almost all of 'Chinese' Wilson's seed was male. The male of the species is totally rampant. There was only one solution. He laid his hands on two females and planted them within tempting distance, to slow him down. The kiwi took off in the opposite direction over the roof of the summerhouse ... the first homosexual plant on record.

With just days to go until the end of filming, there was something missing, but we didn't know what. Could it be palm trees?

We had two prone yet living palms, victims of the bulldozer that had pushed the farm track through to the parkland. Having moved dozens of palm trees in California, Philip assured us that it was a piece of cake. However, they were unbelievably heavy, needing four strong men to lift each one. Holes were dug and the trees were installed, while on the other side of the pool the last lick of limewash was going on the walls of the summerhouse. Somewhere on the road in his white van, Rob was racing back with a statue of the correct period that he'd borrowed from a friend's garden.

There was only one camera angle that would make the Italian Garden look finished. It would involve the cameraman performing acrobatics in the name of art, with the kiwi fruit in his ear. Rob and the statue arrived.

Welcome, Stephanie. Welcome, Stefan.

Action!

Chapter 5

AN EASTER OPENING

O ur ambitions had focused for six months on one thing only: the completion of the work planned for the *Gardeners' World* documentary. We had moved heaven and a great deal of earth, not to mention huge palms and rhodo-dendrons, just to achieve this end. In his concluding commentary for the now famous ten-minute sequence on Heligan, Stefan Buczacki reflected that our project might be an interesting one to watch out for in years to come. His words were broadcast on BBC2, throughout the British Isles, in the autumn of 1991. From then on, we were on the map. Even now, casual visitors to the area pass by the garden entrance, spot our unambitious sign and, recognizing the name from somewhere, feel compelled to come in.

We ourselves had gathered to watch the programme on a specially installed television in the bar of the Llawnroc in Gorran Haven. We waited in nervous anticipation and after-wards felt very proud. Perhaps the biggest surprise was that the programme gave the project real substance in the eyes of friends and neighbours who hitherto had looked upon it with the sort of benevolent condescension usually reserved for the mentally unstable. It is a strange reflection of our times that it took television to make it credible for so many people.

What the programme did was to bear witness to those first random stirrings at Heligan which signalled a return to the land of the living. Almost by chance, it captured that mood of rebirth in the gardens. In truth it was more a case of an army of frogs than a fairytale prince whose awakening kisses brought the hint of a blush to the cheeks of our sleeping beauty. The main body of the garden still lay dormant, but as the pall of eternal slumber was lifted from her, we sensed the return of her own deep, steady pulse and found to our joy that warm blood still coursed through her veins. The more we cherished her, the more exhilarated we felt. The prospect of new life was somehow reflected back, touching us as well. We succumbed to her spell.

John Nelson kept his own counsel and rarely showed any emotion save a grunt of satisfaction at a job that met his own exacting standards. His addiction to the physical endurance of never-ending days on site, no matter what the weather, was a symptom of his devotion. He never seemed to tire, driven on by his obsession to a series of ever-more-remarkable achievements. John's relationship with the gardens became very personal; no one else could ever match his commitment. He pretended that the opinions of outsiders were of no significance. What this meant in practice was that if you weren't a believer, you didn't exist. John could have stepped straight off the pages of a Joseph Conrad novel: a complex character, privately raging against the deck of cards the world had dealt him thus far, yet on the outside patiently chipping away, seeking salvation through sheer hard work. There is a phrase he uses which holds both the wisdom and the ambiguity of a soothsayer's reading of the entrails: 'The tide comes in twice a day, don't ever forget it.'

A Cornishman and intensely proud of it, John was born in Lamorna, in the far west. He moved to London at an early age, which is how he explains the South London accent that belies his origins. His father and mother ran the catering at Stansted Airport and he himself served his apprenticeship as a sheet metal worker in the aircraft industry. A spell of National Service in the 31st Training Regiment of the Royal Artillery, based at Rhyl in North Wales (23615077, sir!) saw him rise to the rank of sergeant major, when he combined the role of driving instructor with square-bashing raw recruits. This period in his life was to leave a deep impression on him. Like many who went through National Service, he learned to take people as he found them – respect had to be earned. He also developed a working philosophy which was to serve us well at Heligan. John is a hard taskmaster: his words of praise are as rare as hen's teeth (although he's softened a little recently), but his saving grace is that he will never ask anyone to do something that he wouldn't be prepared to do himself. The only exception is a call upon craftsmanship outside his sphere.

After the army he went into the building trade, working mainly on old timbered buildings in the Saffron Walden area, where he lived. In these years he gained the skills and sympathy for traditional building techniques which were to prove invaluable to us at Heligan. For a while he became a travelling man as a site construction manager for F. W. Woolworth, building their supermarkets all over England. As the novelty wore off, he felt the draw of Cornwall once more. He returned to make a home in Mevagissey, where he earned a living first as a fisherman and then as a merchant seaman. He plied the coastal ports from the Baltic to northern Spain, until he came full circle and decided that it was time to settle down and turn his hand to building again. And that was how we came to meet – beneath the chimney at Treveague.

What of me? My low boredom threshold and butterfly mind ought to provide the recipe for disaster. However, this mixture is held together by a game-playing mentality that demands challenge and reward. The 'reward' is tempered by an awareness that, but for my unquenchable optimism, would surely have led me to despair: I am cursed with an inability to gain satisfaction from reaching my goal. Maybe it is because I want too much. All my achievements – in sport, in exams, in my career in music where the rewards for success were material as well as artistic – left me feeling hollow. I wanted a hit record more than anything in the world. And yet I remember walking along the Champs Elysées in 1983 with records at No. 1 and No. 2 in the French charts, staying in the Princess Suite of the Plaza Athénée . . . and feeling utterly miserable. Financial rewards had the same effect, robbing most material desires of their symbolic power. Success as an event had always left me feeling lonely and sad, as if suddenly bereft of a good companion. The saying: 'It is better to travel hopefully than to arrive' was composed by a fellow voyager. Perhaps this explains something of my commitment to Heligan, for here is a quest with no definable end, littered with sorties and minor engagements to seize the interest along the way; and with no need to say farewell.

Rob Poole's involvement was different again. He continued working at Newquay Zoo and enthusiastically gave his free time to his new hobby. With a practical, unsentimental outlook on life, he soon carved out for himself a role as site quartermaster. When he and his girlfriend, Suzie Stafford, decided to rent Palm Cottage, the recently restored former head gardener's cottage on the estate, this was deemed as serious a commitment as he could afford to make. Whatever our current need, Rob was the man – not least for a hot toddy pick-me-up after a wet day outside.

Heligan's old camellia collection brings very early spring colour to the gardens, but to this day many specimens remain without a name.

Miniatures of the Tremayne Family

1 The Rev'd Henry Hawkins Tremayne (Squire 1766–1829) was responsible for laying the foundations of the garden, its shelter belts, rides and walled gardens

2 Harriet Hearle, wife of the Rev'd Henry Hawkins Tremayne

3 Mrs Hearle, mother of Harriet Hearle Tremayne

4 John Hearle Tremayne (Squire 1829–1851) began the large scale planting of exotic specimens up the Main Drive and around the Northern Gardens

5 John Tremayne (Squire 1851–1901) carried on this tradition and began to develop the Jungle

6 Mary Charlotte Clotworthy, wife of John Tremayne

7 John Claude 'Jack' Tremayne (Squire 1901–1949) created not only the Alpine and Italian Gardens, but also developed the Jungle into what we know today

Heligan House enjoyed a superb view down into Jack Tremayne's sub-tropical paradise (top). Importing plants and livestock were equally fashionable – and as ever, incompatible. An emu is chased from the lawn outside the house c.1918 (above), during the time it was used as a shell-shock hospital for convalescent officers.

The discovery of the hydraulic rams was one of the high spots of the restoration. Buried deep under the mud, in a valley more than a mile away from the gardens, they were capable of pumping water to a height of three hundred feet at nine gallons a minute, filling a reservoir at the highest point in the garden – which became the water supply for both house and garden from 1880. This fantastic feat of Victorian engineering (opposite) was restored by the same company who built it in the first place and even more unbelievably, the spares were still available.

The rams enabled Jack Tremayne to make a cascading stream the centrepiece of his newly constructed Alpine Garden (top) which we now call the Ravine. We discovered the original stop cock which governed the water flow and made it operational again in what has now become a shaded fernery.

The gentle melancholy of the Northern Gardens is set off by a number of simple romantic structures which we uncovered early on in the restoration. The Crystal Grotto (top) and Wishing Well (above) were swamped by fallen leaves, but otherwise intact. In the spring (opposite) the focus of the pleasure grounds remains Flora's Green, surrounded by historic flowering shrubs, while in the Jungle the top lake becomes a sea of petals.

At the beginning of each year, the Jungle starts to sing with new life. From a frosted, dank valley floor sprouts fresh green skunk cabbage (*Lysichiton americanus*) with its rank perfume (opposite). And while the branches of our native trees are still bare, giant rhododendrons are clad in crimson again and the avenues of Chusan palms (*Trachycarpus fortunei*) stand proud (above) to greet another season.

This original stock of giant rhubarb (*Gunnera manicata*) emerges from a stone-edged swamp; its appearance and annual growth are dramatic with spiky leaves up to six feet across.

In Cornwall snow is a rare visitor and arrives when it pleases – (top in the Jungle) on Valentine's Day 1994 and (above on Flora's Green) over Easter 1998.

Our own native wild flowers are well able to look after
themselves in the glamour stakes.

It became clear that his experience in running the zoo would stand us in good stead when he started to raise issues about managing an 'attraction' which neither John nor I might have considered until it was too late; things like security, basic health and safety precautions and the provision of insurance.

During 1991 we acquired a fourth partner in the project. Roger Noyce ran an excellent plant centre high above the nearby village of Pentewan. Philip McMillan Browse, who was by this time acting as our horticultural mentor, was concerned that many of the fine specimen plants at Heligan appeared to be on their last legs. If the species were to be saved for the future, they needed to be propagated soon. On his advice we sought out an established nurseryman. Roger was enthusiastic and after several visits he asked to join us as a fully fledged partner in the venture. We were somewhat taken aback, but on reflection saw many advantages in having a full-time plantsman on the team. Soon Roger and his two sons were on site at every opportunity. They worked hard with the clearance teams and then undertook a programme of emergency replanting. Roger also took a large number of cuttings to bring on at his nursery.

After the *Gardeners' World* broadcast, the pace grew hotter. The programme exposed Heligan to a wide audience but left us completely unprepared for the ensuing clamour of interest. Everything arose from a single sin of omission. Stefan neglected to mention in his fulsome piece to camera that the gardens were not yet open to the public, nor were they yet remotely capable of being so.

It all started in November. First it was a trickle of curious people who had made enquiries locally and dropped in 'while passing'. It was pretty difficult just to drop in. Heligan was more a building site than a garden. What to others might have conjured up a vision of hell was home to us. Littered with debris, mountains of timber and oozing mud, it had also become a collection point for our treasures: piles of reclaimed materials, from cast iron guttering and downpipes, slates, old glass and large beams to a rather doubtful-looking Land-rover – all donated by supporters of the project. To get as far as the garden proper was an achievement in itself. John and I were flattered by the attention and, amazed that the chaos offered no deterrent, would take time off to give small tours to interested individuals. The word spread that there was something going on and before long we 'welcomed' our first coach into the works area, with a party on board who demanded to see the gardens and wouldn't take no for an answer. Other people seemed to be gripped by Heligan just as we were.

We hadn't given much thought to setting a date when we would open to the public. One thing is certain: it had never occurred to us to open up while we were still in the early days of excavation and restoration. However, the depth of interest being shown encouraged us to look at ways of sharing the experience as soon as possible, without distracting ourselves by trying to provide any but the most basic visitor facilities. This would be part of Heligan's charm. Tony Hibbert then landed us deeper in the mire by bringing a party of fifty members of the Trebah Gardens Trust for a sneak preview, in the course of which he announced that we would be opening soon. We ventured everywhere with the party, even into the Jungle, under conditions which would have given any health and safety officer a seizure. Afterwards Tony was unrepentant and urged us to attempt an Easter opening. He followed this up by sending every journalist who visited Trebah straight on to Heligan, telling them that this was their chance to discover the finest gardens in all

Cornwall before anyone else. Soon the stories started to appear in the press and we had as much chance as King Canute of stopping the inevitable.

The clearance continued at a frenetic pace. The main network of paths was nearly cleared, with the bulk of the work being done by our resident volunteers, occasionally assisted by BTCV working groups. One day John's dog, Fly, got lost in the undergrowth and began creating a fuss, so that the crew downed tools and searched for her. The path was blocked by the usual laurels and some fallen trees, but by weaving in and out of the boughs we made rapid headway into an area we hadn't explored before.

We were close to the north-eastern edge of the garden. Along the boundary wall grew another rampant laurel hedge which had spread in all directions. Underneath its towering branches, we came upon a lovely little brick summerhouse, with three arches hidden behind a curtain of bramble and ivy. The whole scene looked like the most romantic Pre-Raphaelite stage set you have ever seen. The roof was off, and the remains of the wooden seat which had once lined the walls lay rotting on the floor. Trained camellias hugged the arches like sentinels at the gates of Arcadia. They had been dead for many years and, dry as dust, they crumbled to the touch. All that was needed to complete the picture was an angry sky with a shaft of sunlight breaking through to spotlight star-crossed lovers in the ruins. Orlando, with his girlfriend Julie (who had by this time left Slapton Ley to join us) used chainsaws to cut their way through and allow us a closer look. Inside, the limewashed walls were mildewed and flaking and here, underneath the fallen roof, we found a beautiful cobble and brick floor of simple geometric design.

The Northern Summerhouse, as it became known, was the second structure we restored. I found a grant and Sue

Pring, the landscape architect, drew up a plan from which to work. There was no reference to its construction in the estate records, although it is clearly shown on a plan of c.1770. It appeared to be the ultimate destination of the oak-lined Eastern Ride from Heligan House. One would not normally have built a north-facing summerhouse, but this location afforded one of the finest views on the estate. On a clear day – surprisingly rare in these parts, where either fog or heat haze fight for the chance to obscure the view – one could see beyond the Gribben Lighthouse as far as Dartmoor. Looking south one would, at that time, have enjoyed uninterrupted views down the valley over the fishing harbour of Mevagissey. The laurel hedge which had sheltered the building and surrounding gardens from the fierce easterly winds was reputed to have been fourteen feet high with three viewing windows trained or cut into it.

We cut the hedge back to its original boundary line but the branches were left at the height they had reached, creating a mysterious effect and still shading the whole area. John reroofed the summerhouse and repaired the floor, while we deliberated over whether to cut the laurels down and start again. Opinion was fiercely divided. This unfortunately resulted in a falling out with Roger Noyce, who saw it as the straw that broke the camel's back and subsequently resigned. Roger and I have long since made our peace and can now, if somewhat wistfully, laugh about our differences. The laurel hedge in front of the summerhouse was eventually grubbed up and replaced by one of *Griselinia*, a fast-growing, more salt-tolerant shrub from New Zealand. The 1990 hurricane had done too much damage to the shelter belt beyond for us to be indecisive. The garden was now terribly vulnerable to easterly, salt-bearing winds, which would injure the magnificent rhododendron collection, planted long after the summerhouse was built. For further protection we erected four telegraph poles in the parkland and temporarily strung an incredibly ugly but highly effective plastic windbreak between them.

Rob's girlfriend Suzie kept goats. They lived in a well-appointed goat shed. We decided that it was far too good for them and we turned them out. The shed was dismantled and brought to the location we had selected for our garden entrance. Re-erected, it would be pressed into service as a makeshift ticket office. It had wooden walls, a tin roof and a dirt floor, but compared to everything else on site this was luxury. The fact that it had no electricity or running water was a minor drawback – nothing would prevent it from being the most welcoming shack in the county.

Rob set about finding some toilets for us. We knew we couldn't afford anything civilized but even John, with all his experience of roughing it, blanched when a truck pulled up carrying two Portaloos that had been thrown off a building site. They were a present, the only expense being their weekly emptying.

In the rush towards opening we gave ourselves one final task to complete. At the same time that John was working on the summerhouse we decided to restore the great lawn close to our entrance – Flora's Green. We felt that at the very least the public should see its surrounding rhododendrons set off to full effect. The 'lawn' had a concrete road cut into it and large areas were heavily compacted. Rumour had it that the American army had used the lawn as a tank park. The officers had been billeted in Heligan House during rehearsals for the D-Day landings on Pentewan beach, which was reputedly similar to Omaha Beach in Normandy. The ordinary soldiers had camped in the neighbourhood. At the end of the war, a fortune's worth of vehicles and machinery had been buried in specially dug holes on the estate, to save on the cost of transporting it back to the United States – or so we were told. The same story can be heard in every pub along the south coast near a former American base.

We dug up the concrete, brought in topsoil to replace it and ripped up the whole lawn. The earth was turned to a fine tilth and we seeded it at great expense . . . Then it didn't rain for four months. We have a picture of the garden taken from the air in the summer of 1992 by Dave Burns, who rashly volunteered to go up as a passenger in a microlight. Flora's Green was brown as a nut and would remain so throughout our first season.

On the night of April 2, 1992 we suffered a cruel blow. A vicious wind got up and funnelled through the garden, completely uprooting one of the finest rhododendrons on the main Western Ride and ripping some massive branches off the trees. The rhododendron was found the following morning, keeled over with all its roots in the air. Miraculously, although it had fallen on top of one of our highly prized palm trees, it had done no damage. The palm was poking through the rhododendron foliage as if they had been growing together all their lives. There was no way that we could lift the rhododendron upright again, so we decided to make a feature of it, leaving it where it had fallen. We brought in half a dozen loads of fine loam to bank up its roots and planted ferns in it. It was soon to look as if it had been like that for years. The extensive damage elsewhere on the estate had made us question whether we should open the gardens at all, but on April 3 we finally received the lease from the trustees, ready for signing, and this renewed our enthusiasm to drive on with our plans.

★

Good Friday, April 17, 1992 was an exceptionally grisly Easter day. The official opening day of the Lost Gardens of Heligan was the date when all the outstanding jobs were supposed to be completed. John's new seat in the Northern Summerhouse had had its final coat of dark green paint the day before but stubbornly refused to dry, leaving it a sticky threat to unwary visitors. Recently delivered hard-core still lay in mounds around the car park, there were no drinking vessels to accompany the precious bottle of bubbly and, worse still, one of the directors had gone missing. Well past the last minute Rob appeared round the corner at Pengrugla equipped with the most essential item: from a shop in Mevagissey he had managed to scrounge a length of yellow ribbon, which we hastily strung from our new entrance. We elected Orlando and Julie to do the honours, to the applause of a small, proud group of participants and well-wishers. Apart from our own families and the Prings, there was Nigel Mathews from County Hall, and a handful of volunteers. We called the press but I don't think anyone came. A few speeches were made and then we retired to the goat shed for the slicing of the ceremonial 'cake'. Sue Pring had produced an extraordinary marzipan model depicting the life of Heligan in vivid food colouring. Everyone was curious to know who was supposed to be having a passionate fling behind the sugar hedge, and who was flat on their back in the middle of a field and why. There was a moment of great excitement when our first visitor arrived. In fact we were so pleased to see him that we let him in for free.

All was now well. We were properly open. We had been to the bank that morning to purchase change, and brought it back like swag in big cotton bags that weighed a ton. This daily ritual was to govern our lives for a while, and because cash was so short someone always had to ride shotgun into town to make sure we didn't get mugged. We had a little cashbox for taking the money. In the goat shed a voluntary rota for receiving visitors was established between the wives and girlfriends. The Portaloos were now fitted with elsan buckets and water squirters so that you could wash your hands. Unfortunately they didn't work properly and ended up squirting you in the eye or just trickling down your leg, leaving men in particular highly embarrassed. Later that first day, when it started to rain like a monsoon, we couldn't hear ourselves talk for the pounding on the tin roof, and slowly but surely one corner of the shed began to seep and the dirt turned to mud.

Thankfully the opening was a low-key affair, but the way in which visitors turned covetous eyes on the staff thermoses of coffee and tea left us in no doubt that we were going to have to provide refreshments as soon as possible. John's wife Lyn persuaded Rob to rent an urn and before long measures were being taken to turn the goat shed into a tearoom. The lack of water meant that every morning Suzie had to fill two of Rob's large plastic brewing buckets at Palm Cottage and transport them up to the entrance to last us through the day.

Soon after the opening, we had another BTCV working weekend and decided to clear a path from the entrance down through the western shelter belt to provide access to the Jungle. Here John had built a short run of steps and a bridge to take visitors into the tropical interior. Then we had our first complaint. A smart lady in high-heeled shoes with matching handbag walked grandly off in search of the Jungle. She returned in a state of high dudgeon, her shoes spattered with mud, convinced that the whole thing was a joke. She insisted on having her money refunded. In the circumstances we felt foolish relaying to her the plaudits of others, but decided to install a visitors' book soliciting comments from the public. After five years its many volumes attest to the great pleasure Heligan offers to those who pass through its gates.

A few weeks after we opened we had our first attack of vandalism. When you become the victim of senseless damage it leaves you feeling dispirited and angry. One afternoon an old lady came up to the ticket office in some distress, saying that she had been stuck in the Jungle because four teenagers had been smashing up the steps and she was unable to get back. Amazingly she had had the presence of mind to take a photograph of them, which she let us have. We recognized the culprits and went to see their parents.

There was a real danger that we would have to close down for a while after this attack. John was beside himself with rage and determined that nothing would get in the way of our progress. He grimly gathered his tools together, found a new wick for a beaten-up hurricane lamp and set off into the dusk. After working right through the night, with only the owls for company, at daybreak he emerged looking bleary-eyed but triumphant. We were back in business.

Part Three

ACTS OF MEN

Chapter 6

DRAWING BACK
THE VEIL

Historical research has always had a romantic hold over
me. As a teenager in Holland, making a slow recovery
from glandular fever, I spent hours poring over original
Dutch East India Company documents in the vaults of The
Hague Museum. The thrill of turning the dusty pages, some
of which hadn't seen the light of day since the eighteenth
century, filled my head with dreams of buried treasure – and
gave a purpose to my new passion for diving. I built up a
comprehensive database of shipwrecks and their contents;
but alas, the only treasure I ever found was a stolen bicycle in
the murky waters of the River Wear under Prebends' Bridge,
while I was studying archaeology at Durham University.

Heligan's discovery therefore rekindled an old passion, and
one that wasn't tainted with the mixed motivations that fire
wreck hunters. From the beginning we were aware of the
heavy burden of responsibility that came with the territory,
but we seemed blessed with great good fortune. Soon after
our first reconnaissance of the gardens, I was introduced to
Ivor Herring, a local historian and former headmaster, who
had bought one of the earliest flats to become available after
the sale and conversion of Heligan House. Whatever he may

have thought of me, or of the plans that were unfolding to upset the tranquillity of his environment, he generously offered us the fruits of his long researches into the history of the house, the garden and the Tremayne family, whose home he now occupied. Without Ivor's help, the restoration might never have begun. It would have taken us years to wade through the more than three thousand documents in the vaults of the County Record Office in Truro. Instead, we began with the meticulously researched articles Ivor had written. He also gave us some notes he had made from the works of antiquaries and garden enthusiasts who had visited the gardens from the eighteenth century up to the 1950s. From these he had abstracted all references to plants seen in the gardens, and added his own observations on those that remained.

A carefully structured research programme formed the basis for the clearance and subsequent restoration work. It needed to be always several steps ahead of the work on the ground. As much damage could have been done by well-meaning ignorance as by malice. An overgrown garden may conceal many vulnerable plant treasures, only a machete's blade away; and its sudden and imprudent clearance could easily upset the delicate micro-climate within, putting it at the mercy of the elements. The phrase 'act in haste, repent at leisure', is never more apt than in a garden.

Ivor Herring gave me copies of two plans of the estate: one drawn by William Hole, dated 1777, and the other by Thomas Gray, dated c.1800, both prepared for Squire Henry Hawkins Tremayne. They illustrate proposed improvements to the estate, although it is not entirely clear to what extent these plans represent the existing landscape as opposed to the suggested improvements. We added to this collection the first edition 1809 Ordnance Survey map, the 1839 tithe map and the 1881 OS map. By 1881 the estate had reached its zenith and all the important garden and landscape features were present. All the plans and maps show the rides through the shelter belts to the north of the house: one to the east, the other to the west, connecting to create a circular route on the inner edge of the garden boundary. Despite inconsistencies, which no doubt reflect the degree to which each earlier plan was implemented, the main shape of the garden as we now know it was in place by the time the 1839 tithe map was published. These plans and maps provided the foundations for our restoration.

The present gardens at Heligan mirror the enthusiasms of each succeeding generation of the Tremayne family, from the late eighteenth century onwards. The basic shape was described in the 1777 William Hole plan, and the subsequent development of new ornamental garden features and the walled garden complex took place within these confines. The Jungle garden, to the south of Heligan House, was a notable exception. This was specially created in the mid-nineteenth century to satisfy the current fashion for exotic plant introductions. The only other structural modification to the estate came in the early 1830s, with the construction of a spectacular two-mile approach road to Heligan House, called the Long Drive. Although it had great visual impact, the primary reason for its construction was to allow horses with heavy loads, mostly of the newly required coal, to gain access to the house. The traditional route up the steep incline of Pentewan Hill, down through Old Wood and climbing the medieval sunken road was from then on to fall into disuse.

In the course of our research Sue Pring spent months in the Cornwall County Record Office and I followed up leads in dozens of places, including other County Record Offices and the Public Record Office, Kew. Despite there being a vast quantity of documentation, we turned up precious little new information on the gardens and their design. Damaris Tremayne volunteered that there had been a flood in the Steward's House at Heligan, where she believed many of the estate papers had been lodged; and at the Devon County Record Office – potentially important because the Tremaynes had had another country house at Sydenham in Devon – staff reported that all their Tremayne papers had been lost in an air raid in 1942, when a direct hit by a German bomb had destroyed their archive library. As if this wasn't bad enough, it was rumoured that any papers which had escaped the depredations of the war were sold as a bulk lot in an auction at Heligan in 1949. It was believed that these had subsequently been burnt for fuel. Whatever the truth, no planting records or further design details were forthcoming. We did, however, have one piece of luck. Some days after the *Gardeners' World* broadcast I received a letter from the archivist at the North Devon Record Office at Barnstaple, saying that they had recently had a considerable number of Heligan documents lodged with them. There had been no reference to Heligan's location. All the archivist knew was that it wasn't in Devon. It turned out that the estate's former lawyers had their head office in Barnstaple and had recently moved to new premises, which had precipitated a mass clear-out. Any documents of historical interest had been dumped at the Record Office. The Heligan papers included ledgers and invoices, mainly from the late nineteenth and early twentieth century, but to us the most valuable items were the head gardener's work books of 1914–16. There, in three bound volumes, on double-page spreads, were the week-by-week job allocations with names beside them, and a monthly summary of wages – a priceless link with the past.

On the ground, our starting point had to be the clearance of the paths. Until we had a discernible shape, all attempts at a survey would be fruitless. Using the tithe map as our guide, we found the paths by inserting steel rods all over the site until we hit a hard layer under the loam. The rest was relatively easy. Under the close supervision of plantsmen, we sent in teams of 'bramble bashers'. Working in pairs, one would slash with a machete while the other pulled the debris out with a pond rake. If they hit a fallen tree, the chainsaw team would come in and cut a way through. Once a long stretch had been cleared of overgrowth, the dumper truck was summoned. Specially sharpened spades cut along the outside edges of the newly discovered paths, until they bit into the gravel below. Then large forks were inserted on the horizontal and twisted round, as one would wind spaghetti on to a fork. The loam covering, which varied in depth from six to eighteen inches, was held together by the roots of bramble and ivy, so that on twisting the fork it rolled up like a carpet. The roll would be cross-cut every six feet and then lifted into the dumper truck. One of the most exciting days of the restoration was June 5, 1991 when we had a BTCV working group with us, and in a single day we cleared over one hundred yards of the main ride.

After the path was swept clean of dirt, it looked pristine, as if we had dreamed everything. In more than three miles of path clearance there was no visible sign of damage whatso-ever, except where an over-optimistic badger had vainly tried to dig a sett. When I talked with Fred Varcoe, the for-mer head gardener, I mentioned the fine condition in which we had found the paths. He told me that every autumn the gardeners would be sent down to the beach at Pentewan, to collect sea sand at the point where the river meets the bay.

This slightly salted sand was then sprinkled on all the paths, its salinity enough to discourage weed growth, yet not so strong as to damage the plants through leaching.

Once the bulk clearance was finished, a detailed site survey was undertaken. This marked the hard landscape features and the exact location of the trees and shrubs. We entered all the old plans and maps into a computer to create a series of overlays of the same scale, and began the task of unravelling the chronology of the garden's evolution. The Silvanus Woodland Trust then embarked on a survey of all the trees, woody plants and stumps, assisted by specialists in particular areas. The range of plants growing in Cornwall is wider than anywhere else in the British Isles and, as such, poses a technical challenge to professionals unacquainted with the region. Some of Heligan's rhododendrons, because of the complexity of their hybridization, and most of the camellias, because of their early introduction, remain unidentified to this day. Each plant was tagged and identified by a number which was recorded on the main site plan.

The structural changes within a garden are easy enough to trace, from the date they appear on the plans for the first time. However, in the absence of corroborative letters or invoices, it is often impossible to establish when a plant was first introduced. The best one can do is establish the date when a plant was first imported, or sometimes when a plant was first available commercially through local nurserymen.

The overlays revealed, for instance, that what appeared to be a random collection of evergreen oaks was in fact all that remained of the formal avenue which had once lined the ride from Heligan House to the Northern Summerhouse. They further showed that an anomalous pair of old yew trees, growing among a stand of rare rhododendrons, were the sole survivors of a formal yew garden which had earlier been planted on that spot. Imagine our excitement when we plunged our arms deep into the loam of the yew garden and stubbed our fingers on the bases of the statues, still in place. The plates of time, one on top of the other, settling like layers of sediment on the ocean floor, are one of the great attractions of the project.

At this point we began compiling the Restoration Plan for Heligan. Having been greatly impressed by Dominic Cole, a garden historian and landscape architect from London, we decided to appoint him as the leading consultant for its development. A Restoration Plan draws together all the relevant archival information, surveys and plans, to form a policy document on which all future restoration work can be based. It seeks to establish clear priorities and define the ethos of the restoration. Its other main benefit is that, should the principals, God forbid, fall under a bus, others have at least some idea of where to pick up the pieces. Sue Pring worked with Dominic, continuing the research at the County Record Office, while I spent more and more of my time on other things.

The surveys failed to compensate for our lack of planting information. Even the head gardener's work books of 1914–16 had contained little new data of that kind. Inspiration was needed and it came from a most unexpected source. Previously, when working as an archaeologist, I had built up a deep hatred of the anorak brigade, who would descend on sites of archaeological importance with metal detectors and delve through important scientific evidence in a frenzied search for treasure. So when, one evening, I spotted Rob Poole mooching around the paths wearing a set of headphones and swinging a metal detector from side to side, I was a little put out. We talked for a while and he assured me that it was just good harmless fun – his hobby was hunting for old coins along footpaths and new coins on beaches. Subsequently he found some very old coins, one dating from the reign of Edward II and another from that of Elizabeth I. It made us aware that people had lived at Heligan since time immemorial. Even the long history of the gardens was put into perspective.

On one occasion in the garden when Rob had marched on ahead, I heard an excited shriek from the direction of the Mount. A large plum-pudding-shaped pile of earth on the northern side of Flora's Green, the Mount had a little path cut into its side winding to the top. From this vantage point, in time gone by, there must have been a magnificent view. Now, of course, it was completely obscured by invasive laurel. When I reached him, Rob was scrabbling around on hands and knees, digging feverishly. The pinger in the metal detector had made the sound for gold. Rob reached in and brought out a handful of gold wrapping papers, the sort used for Woodbine cigarettes during the First World War. When Heligan House served as a convalescent home, the Mount must have been a favourite place for the recuperating officers to come for a gasper.

The Mount itself had an unsettling appearance. Covered in moss and ferns, it was crowned by two large oaks and a beech tree that had grown in a strange, tortured way. It had obviously been enclosed within the boundary walls when the garden was laid out in the eighteenth century, to make a special feature. At that time it would have been a lookout point, commanding views across St Austell Bay and further east along the coast, almost as far as Salcombe. It was this view that hinted at its previous use. Sue Pring found a reference in the Record Office to a deed for Beacon Field, dated 1623, in which mention is made of an old beacon at the head of it. The 1839 tithe map clearly shows Beacon Field as being adjacent to the wall. If the beacon was old in 1623, it was likely to have been used as an Armada beacon, and probably before that. There are also, however, local myths which refer to the Mount as having been a gibbet during the Middle Ages. Pengrugla, the nearby hamlet, translates as 'the gibbet's head' in Cornish.

The Mount is an important symbol of the way we see Heligan. Where others might have restored it to a formal state – with the trees removed, the face turfed and a neat gravel path winding to the summit – we will not. It would be easily destroyed by the tread of many feet exploring its fragile path. I like the atmosphere it evokes today. The trees have a slightly menacing presence and the moss, ferns and wild flowers look as if they have always dwelt here. It wouldn't take much to remove the trees and tame the Mount, but it wasn't always a garden feature and may indeed once have had a darker purpose. I prefer to leave it in that realm of the imagination which is inhabited by the memory of those who went before us, as well as those whose time has yet to come.

Some weeks later, when I was poking around an old espaliered pear tree that had broken free of its constraining wires many years before, something caught my eye. On the wall, at waist height, was a plant label. The writing was barely visible, so I removed it and took it home. I washed it but left a little liquid soap on the surface – and the writing showed through as clearly as if it had been written yesterday: 'Glou Morceau'. I had an idea. Rob had taught me how to use the metal detector. It was quite sophisticated, with a number of settings to help differentiate between types of metal. An old nail would cause a sharp saw-toothed blip, while pure gold would elicit a rounded bloop. The next day I borrowed it and set out first along the north-facing wall on the outside of the Melon Garden, and then along the inside south-facing wall.

Every twelve feet or so the blip would go, and at anything between four inches and a foot under the surface I found a zinc or lead label. We plotted these on a scale plan and before long we had a large collection, including an almost complete set from the south-facing wall of the Melon Garden. Over a period of a year we completed metal detector surveys of all the 'beds' in the garden. At the time of writing we have hundreds of these labels in our collection, ranging in age from the early nineteenth to the early twentieth century. The survey was more than just an interesting exercise because it has since enabled us to get a picture of the 'wall fruit' production in the walled gardens, as well as giving us a much wider interpretation of the shrub and flower plantings elsewhere.

If you were going to build an estate from scratch, the first things you would need to consider would be the water supply and drainage systems. This only slowly dawned on us. As the research progressed and our regular cross-sections kept finding drains and culverts, our admiration grew for the Georgian and Victorian engineers. The main network of paths had a central drain right in the middle of it, fed at regular intervals by diagonal drains from the sides. The drains themselves were beautifully constructed, using slate bases with bricks on their sides to form the channel and topped with rough stone. The whole was packed down tight with clinker, the waste product from the boilers. The metal detector survey picked up miles of cast iron pipe, which was Victorian, and also another system, of galvanized piping, which we assumed to date from the early 1900s. In the walled garden complex, the metal detector was useless for finding drains and culverts, as the Georgians had used ceramic pipes. The drains in these working areas were crucial, but they had been dislodged and damaged by the roots of the self-set trees, which in some cases had become substantial.

Sue Pring thought that we should try dowsing. I have always been sceptical of this practice and went with her under duress. Taking with us some bamboo canes to mark any findings, we began to lay out a grid of string across the Flower Garden. To my utter amazement, using nothing but a broken coat-hanger, Sue went on to trace the entire length of the drainage system through the walled gardens, down into the Sundial Garden, and from there into the large culvert that takes all the storm water under Heligan House and on, right down to the Jungle below.

In my enthusiasm for this new activity, I asked Sue whether we could have a look in the former Vegetable Garden, to try to pick up the drains there as well. The rods eventually led us into the undergrowth of the former laurel hedge which had once bordered this area. Beyond this lay one of our recent discoveries: the Ravine, or Alpine Garden as it was called at the time of its construction in 1890. We came upon it by falling through a mountain of leaves which had completely filled up its man-made valley floor. More than one hundred yards long and in places more than twenty feet deep, the Ravine is a rockery on a grand scale, with a rough stone path winding through the cleft in its centre. The metal detector survey had a fruitful haul from its slopes, indicating the original character of the plantings there.

The choice of plants was somewhat odd, as it turned out. There is a temptation to accept too readily the quality of past design or construction, as if age was in some way a qualification of merit in its own right. Sometimes I feel uncomfortable in the company of those in the heritage lobby whose regard for the past seems based more on fear of a future for which they feel no sympathy than on a balanced judgement of historic value. Putting the past in aspic can lead to cultural atrophy. There can be few things less fruitful than attempting to restore something that was bad in the first place.

Left to itself the Ravine had created its own magic. Nature had vastly improved the quality of the man-made canvas and we loved it from the moment we came upon it. Large self-set ash and sycamore created a dappled light which suffused everything with a soft glow. There were ferns and primroses in profusion and, in the deeper shade, mosses and lichens provided the backcloth. Climbing up the steep slope one day, John discovered the bed of a stream which ran the full length of the Ravine, culminating in a 'waterfall' which must have splashed down some rugged rocks into a pool. The watercourse was full of leaves but the shape was unmistakable. We decided that we would keep the whole area as a fernery – and resist all calls to restore it to its previous alpine form, on the grounds that it provided the most wonderful atmospheric counterpoint to the blowziness of the main rhododendron lawn, Flora's Green, into which it led.

At the head of the stream, John had slipped and sprawled in the dank loam under a massive evergreen. At first he had let out an oath and then all went quiet until he called me over. There, in the dark recesses of a hole in the roots of another old tree, was a stopcock. We admired the conceit of the Victorian engineer who had wanted to maintain the illusion of nature, by hiding all trace of human hand. On closer inspection we found that a pipe from the stopcock connected to a lead spout set in rock, from which the stream and its cascading pools would have been fed. Another pipe joined the stopcock from underground, where presumably it was linked to the main water supply.

Coincidentally and completely out of the blue, I received

a phone call from a man with an impossibly smart voice. His name was Charles Doble. His firm, Green and Carter from Ashbrittle, near Wellington in Somerset, had put in the original water supply at Heligan in 1880. He still had the receipts to prove it. Not only did he have the receipts, but the remarkable thing was that he still had spare parts for every machine the company had ever built. He was tracing all the firm's original customers, or the current owners of the estates on which the company had once worked, with a view to encouraging them to restore their old water systems to a working condition. Since Green and Carter had been in existence from the turn of the eighteenth century, this was quite a task. Its speciality was the construction of hydraulic ram pump systems, based on an invention of 1796 by the Frenchman Montgolfier, perhaps better known for having invented the hot air balloon. It was soon afterwards, in England, that Green and Carter set up their business.

In the days before mains water, the great estates had to rely on good local sources such as rivers and lakes or specially dug wells. The success of their systems was dependent on both the proximity of the source and their ability to store the water in a clean condition. The hydraulic ram revolutionized the supply of water on many estates. Provided there was adequate flowing water reasonably near, a pump could be operated, using only the power of the water itself. It was completely self-sufficient. Charles Doble felt that the high cost of modern mains water supply, combined with a burgeoning concern for environmentally friendly technology, could lead to a renaissance of interest in the ram pump. The opportunity to meet such a convincing advocate was irresistible.

Some weeks previously, John Nelson, Orlando and Julie had explored a valley to the west of the gardens, in search of a little rectangle marked on the OS map with the word

'Ram' beside it. They had found a curious three-sided wall of stone in the middle of some beautiful, mature woodland. Thinking that was all there was to see, they had come home.

Charles Doble arrived, immensely tall and enthusiastic, in a massive American combat jeep in camouflage colours and bristling with radio aerials, wearing a Gulf War souvenir T-shirt with the inscription 'Bonfire Night Baghdad'. We scrambled down into the valley, which was about a mile from the gardens, and over some forbidding walls into a boggy area. There we found the odd three-sided wall the others had described.

The long narrow walls should have enclosed the access steps down to the ram chamber, but they were filled to ground level with mud. Charles pointed excitedly and said: 'Eighteen feet down, you will find a doorway into a little room, and in there you will find three ram pumps: a two-inch, a three-inch and a five-inch. They are capable of pumping nine and a half gallons of water a minute, to a height of three hundred feet, over a distance of a mile and a half, using only the water power provided by the stream which feeds them.'

We were deeply impressed. We decided to explore further, using a map which Rob Poole had brought with him. This indicated that we were at the merging point of two valleys, each containing a stream. As we headed north, up the hill away from the ram house, we broke through the overgrowth and out into open country, where we came upon a tiny arch-fronted building with a domed roof. Alongside it was a trough.

'This is the catch pit,' said Charles. 'The streams are dammed further up the valleys above us on both sides, and their overflows are directed here, down four-inch ceramic pipes. The water is channelled from here down individual pipes, called drive pipes, which are directly connected to the back of each hydraulic ram pump. The angle of fall on the drive pipes has to be a minimum of forty-five degrees, to deliver the power to the pumps. These pipes are cut deep into the rock below and represent a considerable engineering feat, in an age when the tools were pickaxes and maybe dynamite, rather than earth-moving machinery. There are three levers inside the catch pit, each working a simple on/off valve for a drive pipe, thus giving maximum control on which rams you have in use at any one time. For every nine gallons that go down the pipe, one gallon is pumped. The other eight provide the power and then disperse into the stream.'

Even if the story hadn't been so fascinating, we would still have needed large amounts of water for the garden and the system seemed ideal regardless of its historical interest. To cut a long story short, we managed to obtain some funding from the Countryside Commission to help with the restoration of the rams. During 1992, the ghastly job of uncovering the ram house was begun. The main problem was that the stream which ran alongside the house had broken its banks and filled the house with mud which had seeped in under the walls. First, the banks of the stream were restored. Then the stairwell had to be painstakingly dug out by hand, bucket by back-breaking bucket. The small team, led by Orlando and Julie, worked unbelievably hard. I have never seen people so tired or so comic-strip dirty. Sure enough, the little slate steps revealed themselves, one at a time, until, eighteen feet underground, they stopped at a doorway leading into the ram chamber – which was filled to the brim with stinking mud. Heavy pumps had to be brought in now, as water was gushing through the walls and threatening to flood the whole area. Until the mass of mud was removed, the work had to be carried out in almost pitch darkness, because there was so little room. Eventually, amid much excitement, the team felt the rams under their hands. With the aid of a hurricane lamp they discovered that the little chamber had a corbelled brick roof and there were still some tools hanging from nails on the wall.

Charles Doble's son, Ben, cleared the drains from the ram house back to the leat some way downstream, to stop it flooding. It would be 1994 before the dams were rebuilt and relined, the drive pipes renewed and the rams overhauled. When we watched the giant machine which came to dig out the original drive pipes, we were filled with admiration for the men who had spent eight months installing them in 1880. As Charles had told us, they had cut a massive trench through solid rock, to meet the base of the ram house. When our digger had exposed the pipe run, we discovered that Orlando and Julie had had a narrow escape inside the ram chamber. From outside you could see that water had weakened the structure and the side wall was on the verge of collapse.

The one-inch supply pipe from the rams led back up to the gardens and fed a 40,000-gallon stone-and-brick-built reservoir, set on the highest ground in the garden. This had supplied all the water needs of Heligan House and the adjacent staff cottages, as well as those of the garden itself.

Digging out the ram house and afterwards helping to raise the three enormously heavy brass and iron ram pumps up those eighteen slippery steps was a job from hell. So, when the rams were finally reinstalled and the television crews arrived to witness them working again, it was only fitting that Orlando and Julie should return from Devon, where they now live, to start them up with due ceremony. There was a rush of water and the slow thump began. Up at the top of the garden, a party waited for some minutes before the first dirty water began to belch into the bottom of the newly cleaned-out reservoir; and when it ran clean, we opened a bottle or two in celebration. It is difficult to describe to outsiders how good it felt. It was primitive and private, almost tribal. We now had our own independent water supply – the lifeblood for our garden.

Chapter 7

PORTRAITS ON THE WALL

Some people in Mevagissey still remember the auction of 1949 when, on the death of John Claude 'Jack' Tremayne, most of the contents of Heligan House were put up for sale. Many took the day off to enjoy the gardens and give rein to their curiosity about the Big House. Some came for bargains (of which there were many), while others came to see whether they could obtain a memento of the house that had exerted such a pull over the collective imagination of the village for more than three hundred years. As the crowds dispersed at the end of a long day, bearing their spoils, few would have cared that with the passing of Jack a family that could trace its lineage back to the time of Edward I had lost its last direct male descendant. Now the inheritance would pass down the female line and only through deed poll would the Tremayne name be preserved.

Although the name might survive, the family fortune would not. Short-term measures to save the house merely deferred the inevitable. It was more than thirty years before the family finally admitted defeat and sold the freehold of the house, by which time its maintenance and subsequent conversion had exacted a heavy price.

There is an excellent history of the Tremayne family, transcribed in 1987 by the Cornwall Family History Society. I am extremely grateful to them, because the Tremayne family – for all their enterprise – were arch conservatives when it came to naming their children. 'John' and 'Lewis' recur with enough regularity to turn a researcher to drink. A shockingly high rate of infant mortality adds to the confusion. Up until the mid-nineteenth century it was not uncommon for more than half of the offspring to die before reaching the age of ten and for a previously used name to be recycled within the same generation. Anyone with an enthusiasm for genealogy will find much of interest in the Tremayne history but I shall restrict myself to those family members whose life story has direct relevance to the development of the Heligan estate, save to mention a most peculiar story that occurred around the time that John and Sampson Tremayne moved to the St Ewe area from Lamerton in Devon, thus establishing a Cornish line of the family and an association with Heligan that has endured from 1569 to the present day.

In Lamerton Church, near Tavistock, is a monument to the Tremayne family recording the deaths of fourteen out of sixteen sons and daughters. The remaining two were:

. . . *twin brothers of whom is recorded from good testimony so great a likeness of person, sympathy of affection as can hardly be paralleled in history. They suffered the same pains, awoke and slept at the same moment and no matter what distance they were apart, each brother could tell from his own feelings what was happening to the other. They had a prophetic instinct that they should die together. In the year 1564 they both served in the wars at Newhaven in France (now better known as Havre de Grace) where in this they something differed . . . the one was a captain of a troop of horse, the other a*

private soldier. Being both to the last degree brave they put them-
selves into posts of ye great hazard. At length one of them was slain
and the other instantly stepped into his place and there in the midst
of danger, no persuasions being able to remove him, he was also slain.

On moving from Devon, John had purchased Tregonan, and Sampson had bought Trelissick and, later, Heligan Barton, an old farmhouse at the head of the valley that overlooked Mevagissey. Sampson's son, William, decided to build a hall-house here in 1603, thus creating the nucleus around which the present house developed. He died in 1614, to be succeeded by his son, John, who had married into the wealthy family of Lewis Dart of Pentewan, on whose death he inherited a considerable amount of land in the area. The link is still there on the estate, in the form of Dart's Well, hidden in the undergrowth below the Long Drive to Heligan from Pentewan.

The Civil War brought misfortune to the family. John's son, Lewis, a staunch Royalist, was Lieutenant Governor of St Mawes Castle, and Colonel of a Regiment of Foot in the Royal Army in its western campaigns. Eventually, in 1645, as the Roundheads got the better of events, he retreated to defend Pendennis Castle from attack by the troops of Sir Thomas Fairfax. While the castle was besieged by land and by sea, Lewis's father was taken from Heligan and imprisoned by Parliamentary troops; he was held hostage in reprisal for the alleged maltreatment of parliamentary sympathizers held prisoner at Pendennis. The angry yet formal correspondence across the lines between Lewis and Colonel Richard Fortescue, the Parliamentary commander, in which Lewis points out the illegality of Fortescue's actions, still survives. Pendennis was duly starved into honourable surrender on August 16, 1646 and the next day Lewis was given a pass to return to St Ewe, with his servants, arms, horses and goods. It was signed by Fortescue and William Batten, Vice Admiral and Commander in Chief of the whole fleet. Lewis's house at Kestle, next to Heligan, had been ransacked, first by Fortescue's soldiers, then by soldiers from Essex. His sympathies remained true and soon he was on the run again, escaping to Normandy by boat. He returned to live in exile in Devon for six years, raising money and arms in the Royal cause. During this period he was wounded many times and arrested more; in 1649 his father-in-law was forced to put up a surety of £1000 – a huge sum – against his further offending. Finally, in February 1655, he and his father were summoned to attend the Commissioners for Securing the Peace of the Commonwealth, with a schedule of their estates, which would be forfeited if further offences were committed. After the Restoration, Lewis Tremayne's great loyalty and suffering were rewarded with the return of the Lieutenant Governorship of St Mawes Castle and he was made Vice Admiral for the south coast of Cornwall. When he died in 1684 the family fortunes had revived and he owned properties in more than a dozen parishes as well as tin mining rights.

Lewis's relationship with his son, John, was riven with serious disagreements, which eventually led to their estrangement. When he left home and qualified as a lawyer, John spent all his time at the Inner Temple in London and at his house in Exeter. Even on inheriting, at the death of his father, he never returned to Heligan, leaving the estate to be run in his absence by his mother Mary Tremayne. It was she who, in 1692, extended Heligan to create the William and Mary house that remains today, with a formal garden court laid out around the front. Unusually for Cornwall, the house is built of brick. The bricks were made at the Heligan brickworks – the earliest known in the county. John's only son was lost at sea, so the inheritance passed to his brother, the Rev. Charles Tremayne, and to his son, another Lewis. This Lewis, and his son John, continued the Tremayne tradition of marrying well. Lewis took as his wife Mary Clotworthy, who brought to the family Rashleigh Barton, a fine Elizabethan house in Devon. John married Grace, the heiress to the wealthy St Austell attorney at law, Henry Hawkins. It was John who built the new stables with the clocktower in 1735 and created the parterre gardens on three sides of the house, shown in John Wade's beautiful plan of the same year, before the gardens were expanded into the estate.

Henry Hawkins Tremayne, born in 1741, was John's second son, and so, according to custom, he was groomed for a career in the church. A fine scholar, he was singled out for special mention on the award of his Master's degree at Balliol College, Oxford. He was ordained into the church on Easter Sunday, 1766, and took up the post of curate in Lostwithiel. Within months, his life had changed beyond recognition. His elder brother, Lewis, died unexpectedly and childless, leaving him to become the new squire of Heligan. It is Henry Hawkins Tremayne who laid the foundations of the estate as we now know it. He and his sister Grace were the only surviving family members and they developed a close friendship which would last throughout their lives. Grace remained at Heligan until, ten years later, she married Charles Rashleigh and the newly-weds moved to Duporth Manor, the house specially built for them nearby.

Henry Hawkins Tremayne was a man on whom fortune smiled. He married Harriet Hearle in 1767 and so inherited a third share of the extensive Hearle estates and mining interests. The unexpected death of a cousin brought him Croan Manor near Wadebridge and in 1808, with the death of Arthur, the last of the Devon Tremaynes, he inherited their estate at Sydenham.

The flavour of Heligan in the eighteenth century was perfectly captured in Grace's diaries, four of which – for the years 1774, 1776, 1779 and 1789 – were preserved. Unfortunately they have now disappeared, so I must rely on extracts reproduced in Brian Latham's book *House by a Stream*. The picture they paint is of a life of busy social activity, reminiscent of the novels of Jane Austen. For Grace there was a frantic whirl of trips to other country houses within the Falmouth, Plymouth, Lostwithiel and Bodmin areas. The constant travelling is a remarkable feature in an era when the roads were no more than rutted dirt tracks, for this part of Cornwall had no turnpike roads. The travelling seemed to be concentrated in the summer, with winter conditions probably making the roads impassable. There were games of cards, and dancing both at Heligan and at the Assembly Rooms in St Austell. The guest list at Heligan indicated that at any one time there might be as many as twenty guests for dinner, some of whom would stay overnight and depart, after breakfast, at 10 a.m. The gentlemen would often ride the estate to take in the marvellous gallops in the woods.

Heligan was an important meeting place during this period. Henry Hawkins Tremayne was an active promoter of the political ambitions of Sir William Simon and Sir John Molesworth. Elections at that time took a week to complete and the gentlemen would travel around the polling stations, unashamedly lobbying for support. Grace's diary entries in October 1774 give a vivid impression of the comings and goings on election day:

Oct. 20th – All that came here yesterday went to the election in the morning. Mr Fortescue, Mr John Broad & Mr Hearle breakfasted here & went with my brother to the election. Mr Fortescue & Mr John Broad returned with him & dined here. Young Mr Tredwen, Messrs Dennis, Medling, Rail & Robins from Penryn came in the afternoon. Miss Ball & Miss Nancy Ball drank tea here, Mr Peard absent at the election and returned to dinner.

Sir William and Sir John were duly elected.

The diaries reveal endless lists of visitors, among them local landowners and worthies as well as officers in the army and navy, and businessmen from the mining and fishing industries. Grace mentions regular visits by her physician, a Mr Nicholls, who prescribed cordials against unspecific ailments and, when called upon, also pulled teeth. (The recipes for some of Mr Nicholls's cordials and remedies, written in an almost illegible spidery copperplate, can still be found in the County Record Office.) Another visitor was a 'Mr Clifford (Limner)' – a limner was an artist who made his living by painting quick portraits, travelling from home to home. Later Grace records, 'Sat for my picture to Mr Clifford.' It may be that the one remaining picture of Grace is the one that was executed at this sitting.

Henry Hawkins Tremayne's position as Vice-Warden of the Stannaries, as well as being a mine owner, made him an influential figure within the mining and smelting industry in Cornwall. Though he officially retained his living, he must have needed a willing curate to assist him in his duties. Grace's diaries make domestic references to him preaching, holding prayers and officiating at family ceremonies such as christenings. At the sessions he acted as Judge's Chaplain and he attended workhouse meetings in St Austell. He also crops up in discussions about the construction of the new quay at Mevagissey and at formal dinners in his various official capacities.

The Napoleonic wars had an impact at Heligan, where the neighbourhood lived in constant fear of invasion by the French. Many regiments of Cornish volunteers, financed by the local gentry, were raised between 1779 and 1783. A number of companies went to make up each regiment. Henry Hawkins Tremayne commanded one large company, at St Austell, to which arms were issued on July 19, 1779. The receipt for their return, dated September 30, 1784, is still in existence.

Among his many other interests, the squire of Heligan aspired to create a great garden. To this end he planted large shelter belts of trees to the east and west of the estate. Dissatisfied with the rigid formality of the by then unfashionable parterre gardens that surrounded the house, he set about developing his own ideas.

Sue Pring, researching in the County Record Office, came across a diary written in 1785. It contains a fascinating account of a 'Grand Tour' of southern England, taking in a number of the homes and more particularly the gardens of wealthy and eminent people. From its date Sue assumes the diarist to be Henry Hawkins Tremayne, who would have been about forty-five years old at the time.

His first port of call was the Three Tuns, at Tiverton, where he met with Mr Hole and his nephew. This is particularly interesting as a Mr William Hole, presumably this one, had surveyed and mapped the estate and garden at Heligan in 1777. The Hole Plan shows Heligan prior to the changes imposed after Henry Hawkins's return from his tour. Some features remain recognizable today, such as the shrubbery walks along the eastern side of the Northern Gardens and the top pool of the Jungle, but many of the open spaces within the shelter belts were subsequently to be filled in.

The progress continued with visits to Painshill, Bath and Blenheim. Near Henley, he enthused about Park Place with its subterranean passages, menagerie, temples and 'Rustick' bridge. He moved on to Stowe, Warwick Castle, Coventry, Birmingham and the Leasowes. He seems to have been particularly impressed by precipices, which he noted at a number of places along the way. Near Bridgwater, he visited the eighteenth-century equivalent of a safari park, where he saw birds, deer, antelope and buffalo. Hestercombe, near Taunton, his final stopping point, was the type of fashionable garden to which every man of discrimination aspired.

Now known for its Lutyens and Jekyll garden, Hestercombe was at that time quite different. It had been designed by Mr Bampfyld and was 'small, but laid out with uncommon taste. There is one spot in particular very enchanting . . . a building called the Witch's Cave, composed of Stocks and Roots of trees twisted into the most fantastic shapes. In the division of the octagon [of the cave] is the figure of an old witch with her beard, high crowned hat and broom, in another nick is painted an owl and another a cat.'

On returning home, Henry Hawkins was evidently so inspired by all the fantastic and, more importantly, tasteful layouts he had seen that he set about transforming Heligan. The garden was expanded into the landscape so that the two intermingled, and alterations were made to the house to take account of the wonderful view down the valley. He laid out extensive plantations containing miles of rides around the outskirts of the estate. Folly temples were dotted about in the woods and the walled gardens and shrubberies set out.

The fashionable landscape manner à la Capability Brown had arrived, and by the 1820s Heligan itself had become the epitome of good taste, with visits from travellers extolling its delights. In 1824, Gilbert, the antiquarian, wrote:

The whole of its grounds are rendered delightful by their natural unevenness, deep valleys where the rays of sun scarcely ever penetrate, watered by pooling brooks, enlivened by cascades, are happily contrasted by conical mountains the surfaces of which are covered with lively plantations and adorned with temples. The walks wind over shady precipices and afford agreeable resting places at convenient distances.

Heligan had its local imitators. After Grace Tremayne married Charles Rashleigh and moved to Duporth, they continued to see much of her brother and his wife. The developments in the gardens at Heligan must have made a deep impression on Grace and Charles because their gardens at Duporth, though on a smaller scale, bear an uncanny resemblance. Duporth Manor, now the site of a holiday park, was demolished in 1988 and much of the garden has become overgrown, mirroring the Heligan experience. However, away from the main buildings, covered by overgrowth, one comes across ornamental ponds, rockeries, a grotto and rides snaking into woodlands of fine specimen trees and shrubs, protected by shelter belts.

Henry Hawkins died in 1829 at the great age of eighty-eight, having laid the foundations of the Heligan estate as we now know it. However, the three succeeding generations – John Hearle, squire from 1829 to 1851; John, squire from 1851 to 1901; and Jack, squire from 1901 to 1949 – would each build on what his forebears had created. All noted horticulturists, excited by the remarkable discoveries being brought back from the far corners of the Empire, they were the ones who would develop the plant collections. It was the combination of these characters, the plants and the stage on which they were to perform which would make Heligan unique.

Chapter 8

THE PLANT
COLLECTORS

If Henry Hawkins Tremayne created the structural skeleton
of the Heligan estate as we know it today, it was the next
three generations who would put flesh on to it. By the time
of his death in 1829, all Europe was waking up to the tantalizing possibilities of introducing new plants collected from
the far reaches of the known world. The plant-hunting
expeditions, sponsored by the botanic institutions and the
commercial nurseries, were the subject of much interest and
comment. Their leaders were often feted by high society,
which was not only eager to hear of their adventures but
also anxious not to miss out on the opportunities these
plants might provide. Ironically, in an age associated with the
advancement of science, this passion was as much commercially as scientifically driven, for there were fortunes to be
made by those who could translate the curiosity of today
into the garden plant of tomorrow.

At the dawning of the nineteenth century the lack of
space and poor storage conditions on board ship favoured
collections dried for taxonomic study rather than live specimens; but with each passing decade the balance shifted, until
by the middle of the century the trickle of new plants turned

to a flood. An excited public was waiting with both the desire and, more importantly, the money to experiment with novel additions to their gardens. In most of Britain the majority of the introductions, too precious to be put in jeopardy by the vagaries of the climate, would have been destined for the exhibition glasshouses, stove houses or conservatories. However, in Cornwall, uniquely mild conditions provided the opportunity to develop a spectacular theatre of plants unmatched anywhere else.

With the exception perhaps of Mount Edgcumbe, which is one of the great designed parklands in Britain, the gardens of Cornwall largely eschewed ambitious grand designs in favour of a more understated if somewhat parochial form. Distance from the cultural mainstream is often assumed to be the reason. However, that is to misunderstand the qualitatively different role played by the squirearchy in a remote region. Most of the great families of Cornwall, while having interests and sometimes properties in London, had strong commercial – and social – ties to the local community. The development of mining, fishing, agriculture and local banking necessitated co-operation and partnership with people of different backgrounds, and contemporary diaries make it clear that the class distinctions associated with upcountry landowners were much more soft-edged in Cornwall. In addition, the small population of Cornwall was spread over a wide area. This meant that social activity was concentrated locally, especially in the winter months when the roads were often impassable. It would appear that while social pressure played a part in dampening displays of ostentation, at the same time it made a virtue of horticultural ambition, with its emphasis on good husbandry, a concept understood and appreciated within the wider community.

The writings of visitors and antiquaries provide an idea of

what Heligan was like in the first half of the nineteenth century, before the explosion in planting began. In 1824, shortly before Henry Hawkins's death, Fortescue Hitchens wrote:

Of late years, [Heligan] has been so enlarged and improved by its present possessor, as to assume the appearance of a splendid mansion . . . The trees which flourish around it are sufficiently numerous to shelter it from prevailing storms, without creating a gloom by their spreading branches or concealing from the sight those distant objects which enliven the picturesque scenery by the charms of diversity. The gardens range along the higher ground behind the house; they are cultivated with much care and the hothouses furnish a great variety of curious and aromatic plants.

In the same year F.W.L. Stockdale, writing in *Excursions through Cornwall*, describes the little fishing port of Mevagissey as having 'a romantic appearance . . . with the beautiful mansion and plantations of Heligan forming the background'. Heligan was 'embellished with fine gardens and shrubberies and a pond in one of the gardens had an immense number of gold and silver fish thriving to great perfection'.

John Tremayne, squire from 1851 to 1901, wrote an essay entitled 'Recollections of My Childhood'. At once charming and highly informative, it paints a picture of life at Heligan from just before the death of his grandfather, Henry Hawkins, to the 1840s. It describes his early life, when he studied at home with his two brothers and a sister. A tutor rode out twice a week from St Austell to teach the rudiments of writing and arithmetic. In the early 1830s, he says his father, John Hearle Tremayne, 'built the Lodges and made the New Road [the Long Drive]. The fields through which it came at the lower end used to be tilled, and were called the

'Breakheart' hills. In those days everybody grew as much wheat as they could . . .' He recalls that his father stood six feet tall in his stockings and although not clever in the sciences, had a good grounding in the classics, having been educated at Eton. John Hearle was 'a great lover of Shakespeare, having lived in the times of old Kemble, Sheridan, Mrs Siddons, etc., when people could appreciate Shakespeare, and delight in his plays. His excellent judgement, his knowledge of men, his allowance for the weakness of human nature, his long experience in Parliament, and above all his never failing practice of living up to the family motto – *Nam honor et honestas pari passu cum vitae ambularent* – caused him to be loved and looked up to by all who came into contact with him. I do not remember to have seen him out of temper in all my life.' A lifelong teetotaller because he disliked the flavour, he nonetheless kept one of the finest wine cellars in the county.

John Hearle had, his son said, 'an intense love for Heligan and its surroundings. He was fond of his farm, especially of his Devon cattle, of which he was a good judge – of his gardens, but above all of his trees and woods. I can see him now in his brown velveteen coat, sallying forth with his long saw hook and zage-iron to mark or prune his trees . . . About this time my brother Arthur fell into the round pond in the walled garden, but was fortunately howked out by David Sweet with a rake to save him from drowning.'

The young John Tremayne's tuition continued at a loathsome private school at Exmouth, prior to a spell at Eton. In his teens he contracted a crippling bone disease which left him on crutches for the rest of his life, but his essay contains no hint of self-pity. Instead, he fondly describes his early convalescence in Charlestown, in the company of a seaman called Captain Sam, who was instructed to take him to sea every day for his health, no matter what the weather. This instilled in John a lifelong love of the sea and ships.

There was a good deal of smuggling in those days and I am afraid our men did not look the other way when a cargo was run. One night a string of horses, each laden with a couple of kegs, passed up through the lawn, but was overtaken by the coastguard at the upper lodge. A fight ensued and there was some bloodshed, a man called Frazer receiving a smart cut from a cutlass on the cheek. One of the smugglers (I believe a workman of ours named Latcher) was found in bed at Pengrugla, and I rather think was transported. The cargo was landed under the Watch House at Mevagissey. It was expected, and all the coastguard were inshore on the lookout for it.

The workmen were nice simple people in those days — not over scrupulous about the marriage ceremony, or respect for the Queen's Customs — but a hard working and contented lot. They all wore smock frocks — old John Barbury always had a new one every Christmas Day, which he wore invariably in Church until the next Christmas day came, when it became his working suit and was replaced by a new one, with artful needlework in the front. John always sat in the Twelve best men's pew in St Ewe Church, an honour not usually accorded a labourer.

According to his son, John Hearle was an enthusiastic farmer:

Those were the days when the cultivation of wheat and barley was all important. All the farm work was done by oxen. The same names were handed down from one pair to the pair that succeeded them. Here were Brown and Berry, Bel and Dragon, Goodluck and Speedwell etc. A short man called Will Rowe was the chief driver — a man gifted with an extraordinary power of swearing at his bullocks. Michael Johns was shepherd and head labourer. Tommy

Crocker was an old man with wonderful knock knees – he spent his existence in weaving straw rope.

John Hellyar had a stentorian voice which he used to effect when the neck was cut and the cross sheaf was put in. The neck was supposed to be the last sheaf of wheat which was cut. In reality it was a small sheaf of selected ears, adorned with ribbons, which was put in the servants' hall until Christmas day when it was given to the best beast on the farm. All the wheat was then cut by sickles, i.e. reaping hooks. I have seen women reaping frequently. The barley was cut with scythes. Cutting the neck was a great function. Michael Johns held it aloft in his hands and roared out 'I have 'un – I have 'un.' John Hellyar bellowed out in response: 'What have 'e? What have 'e?' Michael replied: 'The Neck – the Neck – the Neck' and then all shouted Hurrah. You could hear this ceremony going on neighbouring farms from quite a long distance.

Our migrations to London were a dreary business. All heavy plate etc. was sent by ship to Toppings Wharf in London. My father and Mother travelled in the yellow chariot and we children . . . in the big yellow Landau which did not open. We took four days about it. The first day to Sydenham [the Tremayne property in Devon], the second to Ilminster, the third to Deptford Inn arriving on the fourth in London. The Landau with four horses, the chariot with two . . . The servants travelled up by coaches – heavy and slow. When my Father and Mother went to town, they hired a house for three months. They did not go every year.

John Hearle Tremayne, who had inherited Heligan from his father, Henry Hawkins, in 1829, married Caroline Lemon of Carclew. He represented the County of Cornwall as Conservative MP for twenty years in five successive Parliaments without opposition and was High Sheriff when the first rumblings of disquiet were heard at the impact of industrial change. John Rowe, writing in *Cornwall in the Age of the Industrial Revolution*, tells of events in February 1831 when there were clashes between workers and mine owners. The Riot Act was read and the men refused to disperse. The ringleaders were arrested and taken to Bodmin Jail. A further demonstration erupted outside and 'The presence of additional special constables and militia there made them ready to listen to the pleas of the High Sheriff, John Hearle Tremayne, for the maintenance of law and order, and they were induced to depart.'

In spite of his busy political career, John Hearle found time to develop the gardens at Heligan. His son John's assertion that he cared most for his beloved trees is borne out by the work that can definitely be attributed to his time. The ornamental plantings down the Long Drive were highly unusual because they featured a new introduction to Europe. Anthony Buller, MP for Liskeard and a great friend of John Hearle's, gave him seeds collected in Nepal, of a small tree with stunning butter-yellow flowers, then called *Benthamia fragifera*, and now known as *Cornus capitata*. John Hearle had the seeds germinated and in 1832 he boldly planted the entire length of the drive with the saplings. They were to develop their remarkable flowers every summer and fruits that looked like lychees. The result was so successful that several years later the *Gardeners' Chronicle* referred to the Long Drive as being one of the finest in the country. Today only a few of the original *Cornus capitata* remain, but from their seed we have brought on replacements and replanted many saplings in their original locations. In summer it isn't difficult to imagine how breathtaking the Drive must have been in its heyday.

Although Humphrey Repton, the great landscape designer, is not known to have worked at Heligan, it is hard to believe that his influence was not felt. Repton designed the superb layout at Antony for Reginald Pole Carew, MP for Lostwithiel, and Pole Carew and John Hearle are known to have been friends.

In September 1841, Barclay Fox of Penjerrick, visiting the Tremaynes with his sister Caroline, wrote of the gardens that they were 'laid out in good English taste, with grass walks and beautiful vistas'. He went on to describe how he and his sister toured the estate on horseback, and 'dived into the deep shade of Heligan Woods, amongst which are some of the finest oaks in the county. After a ride of eight or nine miles we returned to dinner at seven.'

John Hearle's passion for trees probably led him to begin planting the area which we now call the Jungle, the sub-tropical valley garden to the south-east of Heligan House. All the early plans show only one pond at the top, with an area of 'orchard' below it. The introduction of some fine *Cryptomeria japonica* 'Lobbii', discovered by the plant hunter Thomas Lobb in the Far East, probably dates from John Hearle's time. In this period the Cornish Lobb brothers were exploring different continents. William Lobb's early hunting ground was South America, from where he introduced the Chilean *Araucaria araucana*, the monkey-puzzle tree. This became a firm favourite in many of the gardens of the South West, including the Jungle at Heligan.

Although an important botanical collection was established between the early nineteenth and twentieth centuries, neither Heligan nor the Tremayne family played a particularly important part in the history of the plant hunters. That honour must surely go to the Williams family at Caerhays, the Fox family who built some marvellous valley gardens on the Helford River – such as Penjerrick, Trebah, Glendurgan and Carwinion – or the Hawkins family at Trewithen, where George Johnstone assembled one of the finest twentieth-century collections of plants in Britain.

Heligan's significance is for different reasons. It is among the oldest gardens in Cornwall, with many of its plants pre-dating the rush of the late nineteenth- and early twentieth-century introductions and ironically, through neglect, it has retained most of the important plants in its collection, many of which have grown to a great size, cocooned in the overgrowth from which we rescued them. Our experience of discovery, unveiling the garden, was enhanced by a feeling of fellow-spiritedness with those who had brought the original plants back from their travels. Each exotic shrub or tree has an adventure attached to it, and a story to tell. For sheer bravery the great nineteenth- and early twentieth-century plant hunters are hard to beat.

While Captain Vancouver and his ship's surgeon/botanist, Archibald Menzies, were mapping the Pacific Coast from north to south with military precision, David Douglas, a taciturn Scots individualist, was making epic solo journeys through the vastness of western North America. Here he endured great hardships among the native Indians, gaining their respect and thereby persuading them to share the secrets of their sacred places. How ironic that on a respite from plant hunting he should break his return journey from North America with a visit to the volcanoes of Hawaii, only to die by falling into a bull pit, a trap set to catch wild cattle. The extraordinary French missionary and plant hunter Père Armand David, working in China, discovered among many marvellous plants the pocket handkerchief tree (*Davidia involucrata*). He was, incidentally, also the first European to see a panda, of which I am reminded every year when the white flowers reappear on our *Davidia* in the Sundial Garden. Robert Fortune in China, Thunberg in Japan and, towards the end of the century and into this one,

George Forrest – so closely associated with Caerhays and Trewithen – add to the rich tapestry. Who can feel the same way about *Rhododendron sino grande*, when they know that many on the expedition were murdered and Forrest himself escaped only by the skin of his teeth? This isn't a plant, it's an icon. Ernest 'Chinese' Wilson, Farrar, Kingdom Ward – the list goes on and on.

The more I learned the more excited I became, as I began to understand the extraordinary energy of the period. Until I came to Heligan I had little more than a passive interest in plants. Now, viewing them in a historic as well as a scientific context, I am a passionate enthusiast. Philip and I would often talk about our heroes, Darwin, Huxley and Lyell. Working people used to queue up for the public lectures given by Huxley. It is a tragedy that so many people now have lost their sense of wonder.

If I were looking for a fourth hero it would undoubtedly be Sir Joseph Dalton Hooker. Joseph Hooker was one of the giants of his generation. His father was the first true scientist to be appointed director of Kew Gardens and Joseph, infected by his father's enthusiasm, set off to make discoveries of his own. He travelled on expeditions to Iceland and to Antarctica before deciding to mount one of the most exhaustive explorations yet undertaken – to the Himalayas, most notably to Sikkim and Nepal. What was to make this expedition so special was that it marked the first major use of the Wardian Case. In 1834, a medical doctor from Ealing named Nathaniel Ward had accidentally discovered that plants in sealed containers create their own atmosphere and can therefore survive. He quickly patented a box with a lid of canvas – the forerunner of the modern terrarium. It was Hooker who recognized that, because it resolved many of the problems associated with long sea journeys, it had enormous potential for live plant transportation, and he commissioned the construction of a great number of them. Heligan's connection with Hooker stems from the fact that the rhododendrons introduced to Britain by this expedition were soon ascribed the generic name of 'Hooker rhododendrons', and Heligan has one of the finest collections of these in the country.

When John Hearle died in 1851 he was succeeded by his son John, whose childhood recollections began this chapter. John was also a keen gardener, with a passion for hybridizing rhododendrons which he shared with his son Jack. Hooker was determined to establish the Indian rhododendrons in British gardens and dispatched seed and seedlings to south-west Scotland and Devon and Cornwall. It is known that seedlings were sent out in 1851 from Kew. Hooker and Sir Charles Lemon of Carclew were good friends, indeed Lemon had contributed to the expedition expenses. The seedlings undoubtedly went to Carclew, Tremough and Penjerrick, and Heligan's collection came from Lemon to his brother-in-law, John Tremayne.

The plantings enclosing Flora's Green comprise mainly hybrids developed from the Hooker collection, the originals of which were planted down the rides, in the area now known as New Zealand, and between the walled gardens. There were also several against the House, most of which have now gone, and in the Jungle area which John was developing. Fifteen species of Hooker rhododendrons are represented at Heligan, among them *R. arboreum* in several colours, *R. falconeri, R. decorum, R. aucklandii, R. thomsonii, R. cinnabarinum, R. campanulatum, R. hodgsoni, R. grande* and *R. niveum.* The *niveum* in particular is magnificent, but it enjoyed a chequered history as a garden favourite. Its purple colour fell from fashion as a result of its similarity to the first artificial chemical dye to be made commercially available. In the early 1900s it was rooted out wholesale in many of the great gardens through sheer snobbery. Distinguished by its dense globular clusters of flowers, it is something of a rarity today. Some of the most interesting rhododendrons are hybrids developed by John Tremayne. He was one of the first to cross *R. aucklandii* (*griffithianum*) with *arboreum*. The first recorded name of this hybrid was 'John Tremayne', though this was changed later to 'Beauty of Tremough'. A clone was called 'Mrs Babbington', after a daughter of John Tremayne. The blood-red *arboreum* is now uncommon, but there are several at Heligan and the finest cultivar was indeed known in commercial circles as 'Heligan'. It has now disappeared from catalogues, but we hope soon to make it available once more. Heligan also boasts some of Jack's hybrids which have an equally good, blood-red flower.

In the 1890s, after a failed marriage, Jack returned to live with his by now wheelchair-bound father at Heligan and together they put their energies into developing the gardens. Jack took special responsibility for the Jungle, while John's main interests narrowed to rhododendron hybridizing. This was a time when many trees and plants were introduced which would have a major visual impact on the garden as a whole. The large numbers of Chusan palms (*Trachycarpus fortunei*) are a good example. These were brought to Britain, from the island of Chusan in the Yangtse River, in 1849 by the great Scottish plant hunter Robert Fortune. One was planted at Kew, and another was presented (at Fortune's request) to the Prince Consort and planted at Osborne House on the Isle of Wight. Both of these still survive. Later they were to become a key component of design in many of the great gardens of Cornwall. The earliest distribution of these palms in the British Isles dates from 1860, when

Glendinning's Nursery auctioned plants grown from seed collected by Fortune. However, the majority of Chusan palms to be found in Cornwall were probably introduced after 1891, when the horrendous blizzards in April of that year had killed almost all the exotics in the county. At Heligan these palms line all the main rides in both the Northern Gardens and the Jungle.

The other major introduction was the tree fern (*Dicksonia antarctica*). It was introduced around 1880 by Treseder's, the famous Cornish nurserymen, two of whom had set up nurseries in New South Wales in Australia. The specimens would arrive as ballast on the quayside at Truro. The large dry rooty stumps were then thrown into the river to be rehydrated before distribution among Cornish gardens such as Bosahan, Trebah, Trewidden and Heligan. They proved a great success, both commercially and horticulturally. Most of the originals came from New South Wales and they seem remarkably suited to Cornwall's climate.

Heligan probably has the largest collection of tree ferns in Britain — primitive and beautiful relics from a time when dinosaurs walked the earth. They adapted well through the years of neglect and the only ones that have died appear to have had their tops rubbed out by the branches of invasive trees growing next to them.

Jack had a passion for the Jungle. Although he was much influenced by the prevailing fashion for 'Japanese' gardens, he soon developed his own vision, which involved the creation of a wild place containing as wide a range of exotic plants as he could find. His first introductions have been mentioned, but his plant palette was more subtle than mere avenues of tree ferns and palms. He planted swathes of different bamboos to create ever-changing green textures, drifting down to the water's edge. Against this backdrop he planted individual specimen trees and shrubs, or used existing plantings to better effect, so that their foliage or flowers became the focus for a particular vista. It was Jack who added the third pond in the middle of the Jungle. He built a large dam of stone with a waterfall that dropped into an area designed to replicate a swamp, into which he planted large numbers of *Gunnera manicata*, whose giant leaves would grow to obscure all signs of the dam. It is a marvellous confection, set off by views of three of perhaps the finest trees in the garden, each now thought to be the largest known of their kind: a huge *Podocarpus totara* or New Zealand yew, a *Pinus thunbergii* or Japanese black pine, and two magnificent *Cedrela sinensis* (nowadays known as *Toona sinensis*), misleadingly referred to as the Chinese cedar. The larger *Cedrela* blew over in the hurricane of 1990. It is still alive and while it may not now be the tallest, it is certainly the longest in the world.

When we first entered the Jungle we felt like explorers coming on a lost world. Hundreds of self-seeded sycamores and ash trees obscured the landscape. Ferns, mosses and lichens covered everything in this dank place, while here and there the eye was caught by exotic foliage and clumps of bamboo. The trees were so dense that one had only to venture a short way in to get completely lost. It was Stewart Harding from the Countryside Commission who gave us the courage to begin extracting the more recent intruders. We were cautious, not wanting to lose the mysterious quality of the place. However, the Silvanus Woodland Trust's tree surgeons worked with such skill that there was little damage to the shrubs and bamboos growing underneath, and each departing tree revealed more of the original masterpiece.

The restoration of the Jungle required monumental effort, because the terrain is so inhospitable, leaving clearance teams no option but to burn excess timber within the valley rather than risk carrying it out. A photograph of the top lake in about 1880 shows the view across the lake and back up to Heligan House. In the foreground are some scenic swans, and behind one can just make out the shape of a punt. When we found the Jungle, the top pond was completely filled with years of leaves and mud and had become so silted up that it supported a small plantation of willows. We made several vain attempts to clear it by hand before contacting the National Rivers Authority to seek their advice. We asked them for sponsorship in return for television publicity. They came, prodded around, and said that they'd be delighted to help. Two men arrived with a digger and a tracked dumper truck to clear the lake, they said, in three days. Unfortunately, though the NRA men had indeed prodded, they had prodded the area where, in the old photograph, the punt had been moored. The first scoop of the digger revealed the top of the landing stage. Instead of three days' light work in front of the cameras, it became three weeks of civil engineering. To be fair, the NRA took the challenge on the chin. I hope they feel that it was all worthwhile now that the results can be enjoyed by so many.

Because it was impossible to take machinery further down the valley, we decided to put one of our BTCV working holiday groups to the task of clearing the second pond. For several days they dug and pulled and raked, to little effect. For the first time we witnessed a whole team becoming demoralized. Suddenly one of the group, a physicist who had scarcely spoken in the previous three days, came up with an ingenious solution. Using a long tube of corrugated plastic one foot in diameter and a cork to fit it, his system involved the bung being explosively pulled from the pipe in order to create a vacuum. The effect was astonishing. It was as if he had struck oil. The pipe writhed like a snake, with the chap holding on to one end of it for dear life, while the mud launched itself everywhere. In just two days the entire pond was emptied.

As clearance of the Jungle continued lower down the valley, plant identification and replanting commenced. It was imperative to replant the shelter belts on the outside edge of the Jungle, and to re-establish those trees and shrubs with an obvious place in the design. And so we began our own plant-hunting exercise in earnest. We were extremely lucky to be introduced to Ray Townsend, at that time the curator of the bamboo collection at Kew. He and Mike Bell of the Bamboo Society, a good friend of Heligan, have both spent a lot of time identifying our bamboos and helping us to develop a strategy for replanting. Both have been generous to us with plants from their own collections. This tradition of generosity in the plant world takes an outsider completely by surprise. It took me a while to get used to people giving me things with no hidden agendas at all, just a generous spirit and an interest in what we were doing.

We needed replacement tree ferns. They were not only hideously expensive but also at that time incredibly difficult to get hold of. In 1993 we hatched a plan with Tony Hibbert, from Trebah, again with the help of Stewart Harding of the Countryside Commission, and formed a garden consortium to import a container load of tree ferns from Tasmania. Tony had been in touch with an environmental organization over there which was selling mature tree ferns, removed from the path of a logging operation. After lengthy negotiations and much correspondence to establish the correct phytosanitary procedures for introducing plants from overseas, we finally heard that our container was on its way, by sea.

It would have been romantic to watch our precious cargo

being unloaded from a three-masted barque on to the quayside at Falmouth. Instead we had to collect it from an industrial unit near Helston. Even so, we still had the feeling that we were re-enacting a scene from long ago, and it felt very special. We stacked the tree fern trunks on the back of a flatbed lorry and proudly took them home to Heligan. Some went into the Ravine and New Zealand in the Northern Gardens, but most were taken straight down to the Jungle, where they were laid out in the bottom pond to rehydrate. The previous cargo would have arrived in the same place almost a hundred years ago.

Orlando and Julie planted the replacement tree fern avenue, and then we all waited like nervous parents to see whether our offspring would be healthy. Fortunately, following St Swithin's Day it rained for weeks on end and soon the little hairy shoots started to form and slowly uncurl from the matted nests in their crowns. We all breathed a collective sigh of relief. I would like to think that John and Jack Tremayne would have smiled in sympathy.

Chapter 9

THE PRODUCTIVE
GARDENS

There is something comforting about a walled garden. Some of my fondest childhood memories were formed in the snug confines of the walled garden at the home of my English grandparents, Hartford Hall in Cheshire. I remember the excitement of picking pears and plums from the old fruit trees trained against the warm red bricks; and the nearest thing to heaven was playing hide-and-seek among the raspberry canes, under hopeless but strict orders to return with my wicker trug full. The memory of Granny's raspberry preserve still burns brightly; thick dollops of it, smothering thinly sliced white bread and butter, and bringing back, for an instant, the long days of summer.

What is it about a smell that can bring the memories flooding back? The scent of a freshly clipped box hedge — and the walled garden at Hartford comes to life, as an impression more complete than any photograph could give. And moist earth mixed with ferns. How I loved that subtle aroma as I prised up the large red sandstones that lined the walk down to the pond, hunting for toads. Collins, the gardener, had a particular smell. I'm sure it was the hard work. Different from the sour body odour of office types, this was open pored and honest. I always associated it with wisdom, because Collins was the wisest man I knew. His face escapes me now, but the low Cheshire burr and his kindly patience are recalled every time I come across that odour. Anthony Burgess once wrote that his eyes would prick at the mention of the word home. It made him feel lonely. My garden smells recall something good, secure and happy – yet tinged with a sense of loss. My grandfather died and the house was sold and turned into a hotel, its contents auctioned. I recently went back and tried to conjure up the memories, but I could not. You should never return.

In February 1990, when I first came to Heligan, I had wanted so badly to push through that broken wooden door into the walled garden and revisit what lay beyond. I realize now what Burgess meant: I was coming home.

Heligan, like hundreds of similar traditional estates across the country, had been a model of self-sufficiency and envi-ronmental conservation in an age when such concepts would have been no more than accepted practice. The invoices and ledgers found at the Devon and Cornwall County Record Offices show that up until the late nine-teenth century, the estate catered for almost all its own basic requirements. Apart from luxury goods, the only imports were lime, needed as a fertilizer and for building, and coal, to fire the new generation of boilers used for heating the glasshouses in the productive gardens.

The Home Farm, centred on the parkland, produced all the livestock, cereals and bulk vegetables to meet the needs of the immediate community. The woodlands provided mature timber for building, the coppiced areas yielded wood for fencing, bean poles and pea sticks, and charcoal burning was carried out under licence. There were stone quarries, water-driven corn mills, sawmills and even, for a time in the eighteenth century, a brickworks.

The apple orchards grew fruit for eating, cooking and cider making, and extensive hop gardens supplied Heligan's own brewery. A bee-bole wall contained fourteen apsed recesses for sheltering straw skeps. The bees were important in the garden as pollinators for the fruit, and in the house for their honey and wax. The honey was used as a sweetener and for making mead, the wax for candles and polishes.

While successive squires indulged in the design and planting of the pleasure grounds, in the productive gardens the head gardener's word was law. At Heligan these comprised four walled gardens and a vegetable garden growing most of the vegetables and all of the soft fruit, wall fruit, herbs, cut flowers and exotics to supply the needs of the Tremayne family and their guests at the Big House. In the nineteenth century, the head gardener had twenty-two staff under him, more than half of whom worked exclusively in the productive gardens, and the rest worked further afield.

The head gardener was charged with the responsibility of supplying fresh produce throughout the year, which demanded the utmost skill in the arts of forcing and retarding the natural growing habits of crops, in order to extend the harvesting period. He had to be careful also to select varieties that stored well. His choice would be coloured by the needs of the cook, as his daily routine would include a visit to the kitchens at the Big House, bearing a selection of his finest produce. They would discuss her requirements for the following day. Even when the squire and his family were away, hampers of fresh food were sent to London by carriage or, later in the nineteenth century, by train. Herbs and fruits were needed for medicinal cordials. (From the recipes which remain at the County Record Office it seems that the key ingredients were brandy, port and blackcurrant – as if getting drunk was a restorative in its own right.)

The head gardener also supplied floral arrangements for the house. In the winter, spring bulbs would be forced in the dark house for early flowering, while huge quantities of cut flowers would be provided throughout the rest of the year. Exotic collections of stove (hothouse) plants were brought up from the glasshouses as they came into flower, and for special occasions he produced confections of the very finest plants and exotic fruits that the garden had to offer.

The head gardener had a special relationship with the squire. At Heligan, he was in the service of a family with keen horticultural interests, who would have consulted with him about the choice of plants for both the gardens and glasshouses, and about the latest technologies the now burgeoning Industrial Revolution had to offer. There were as many ingenious variations as there were gardens, each attempting to best the other in friendly rivalry and to construct the ultimate pit, glasshouse or boiler. The homogeneity that arose out of the mass production techniques of the Industrial Revolution capitalized on a rich era of experimentation preceding it. The head gardeners of Heligan undoubtedly contributed their own ideas to some of the constructions, even if they were developing practices that they had seen or read about elsewhere. The eighteenth and nineteenth centuries were exciting times for horticulture and many of the great garden owners were feverish in their ambitions to grow ever more exotic plants. By 1824 Heligan was already known for its glasshouses full of 'curious and aromatic plants', building on a tradition begun a century earlier.

In the early days of our restoration, a mutual friend gave me the number of Peter Thoday, who had been the consultant and co-presenter of the BBC TV series *The Victorian*

Kitchen Garden. When I spoke to him he was highly affable and full of useful information, but it was clear from the tone of his voice that he thought I was probably a crank and he politely declined to come and see the gardens. Many months later, after he'd heard that Philip McMillan Browse was on the team, he decided Heligan might be worth a visit.

Under its mantle of self-seeded trees and overgrowth, it was still easy to imagine the Melon Garden as the heart of the head gardener's kingdom. The compact group of working buildings, frames, pits and greenhouses gave it a functional air, even in decay. John and I had come to the view that we should clear the trees from one side of the walled garden and then carry out a series of trial excavations to establish what precisely had gone on here. A BTCV working holiday group joined us to clear the eastern half, with its greenhouse and a long low pit in front of it. The pit was of great age. At the end of its active life it appeared to have been used as an ordinary salad frame, but the first trial cross-section exposed intricate honeycomb brickwork, clearly intended for the circulation of hot air. This was no ordinary construction. The pit was nearly fifty feet long and, when we found it, filled to the brim with earth. On clearance, we discovered that its walls were double skinned, their top four courses of honeycomb brickwork running the length of both front and rear, before giving way to solid brick below. The bottom of the pit was covered with thick slabs of slate which, when lifted, revealed three six-inch-deep channels which appeared to have been used for water. There was evidence that three stone cross-walls had once separated the pit into four compartments.

Peter Thoday's arrival in July 1992 was heralded with a fanfare. He was clearly impressed by the project, and it didn't take long for him and John Nelson to develop a rapport as they investigated the structures we had uncovered in the productive areas. When we explained our ambitions to restore the complex to a working condition he pledged himself enthusiastically to the team. Heligan could be one of the most important nineteenth-century gardens in Britain, he thought, because it had fallen asleep so early on and had not become the victim of modernization. So many places like this had been destroyed, whereas Heligan provided a unique opportunity to tell the story of the real gardeners who once worked here.

John and I were obviously delighted to have Peter's support, but we both winced at the necessity of removing the romantic overgrowth from the entire productive area. It was then that Peter muttered his challenge: 'Do you want to make a greatest hits album, or have you the ambition to play the whole opera?' The gauntlet thrown down, it didn't take John and me long to make the fateful decision to go all the way. Peter and Philip, the two experts, smiled at our naivety but humoured us nonetheless.

That evening Peter addressed the first gathering of the newly formed Friends of Heligan, unexpectedly packed like sardines into the pavilion of Gorran Cricket Club. He wowed them in the aisles with a revivalist's fervour, telling stories from *The Victorian Kitchen Garden*, and the crowd went home converted like initiates of a new cult. I think John, Philip and I realized then that the quest to restore Heligan's productive gardens would appeal to a far wider constituency than we would ever have dreamed possible.

Peter and John were fascinated by the pit in the Melon Garden. Peter's excitement grew as he became convinced that it was a pineapple pit. He had seen drawings of layouts very similar to this in books. On a second visit he introduced us to John Chamberlain, an architect with a passion for the past. John volunteered to make technical drawings of the pit and work out its evolution, as he was convinced that the structure had been developed and adapted over a long period. By dating the bricks in the foundations, John was eventually able to place its first construction in the early eighteenth century. As the months went by I was to learn a great deal about the curious history of pineapple growing in Britain. In the process we enjoyed ourselves enormously and now, to the best of our knowledge, we have the only working, manure-heated Georgian pineapple pit in the world.

It is hard to convey the excitement that surrounded pineapple growing in the eighteenth and nineteenth centuries. At all the main horticultural society shows, the pineapple section would be the centre of the exhibition. The pineapple, *Ananas comosus*, originated in South America, although it now grows throughout the southern hemisphere. It was first introduced to Europe by the Spaniards in 1513, but was not grown in England until the beginning of the eighteenth century. (The fruit shown in the famous picture hanging in Kensington Palace of King Charles II being presented with a pineapple by his head gardener, Rose, is popularly believed to have been imported from Holland.) By 1730, pineapples were to be found in most of the principal gardens of England. Attempts at seed propagation had been largely unsuccessful, so the most popular method involved taking large suckers from the base of the stem of an existing plant or using the crown from a fruit.

Each head gardener had his preferred method for growing 'pines', but when all the posturing is over, it is clearly an easy plant to grow in most soil conditions. The trick lies in maintaining the right balance of water, light and heat. The pineapple could take up to two years to mature and produce fruit. But by the early nineteenth century, writers such as

Thomas Knight, the President of the Horticultural Society, were recording that the largest suckers, when forced with great heat in the early stages, could be fruited in ten months. Thomas Knight was responsible for one of the earliest published designs for a manure-heated pineapple and melon pit (1822), many of whose features are incorporated within the design of the one at Heligan.

There were fewer than a dozen varieties of pineapple in use until the end of the nineteenth century and only five are regularly mentioned in the transactions of the RHS of Cornwall: 'Black Antigua', 'Cayenne' ('Chian'), 'Enville', 'Jamaica Queen' and 'Providence'. The first four were grown for their flavour and averaged between 5lb and 7lb in weight, whereas 'Providence' was a competition pine weighing in at over 14lb, and apparently tasting dreadful.

The excavations of our pit and the greenhouse behind it revealed a complex series of design changes during more than a hundred years of use. In the first phase it appears that there were a pair of fifty-foot by six-foot pits, one behind the other and separated by a central manure trench four feet deep, which ran the length of the buildings. (Only one pit survives.) Similar trenches ran along both outside walls. The trenches contained drainage channels that would have carried off both the surplus water and the 'liquor' from the fermenting manure, to a 'liquor pit' adjacent to the southern gateway. This would have been used as a source of liquid fertilizer. At the base of the central trench lay a six-inch terracotta flue, ducting cold air from the outside into the rear greenhouse, warming it under the fermenting manure as it went. The pit was divided into four growing chambers, intended either to be kept at different temperatures or to grow different varieties in order that they should not all ripen at once, which would have been wasteful. Underneath the slate floor, the three lined evaporation channels would have been water-fed from an external tank. The water was kept at a constant depth in the growing chambers by means of copper syphon pipes, which passed through the dividing walls. The slate floor above would have been covered by approximately fourteen inches of tan bark (the oak bark used in the leather making process) or in some cases leaf litter which itself was fermenting. We now get our tan bark from Croggan's, the leather tanners in Grampound, whose family firm has been in existence for over two hundred years. It would be nice to think they were Heligan's original suppliers. The pines, in pots, were plunged into this.

The optimum growing temperature for pines was agreed to be seventy to eighty degrees, but the heat coming through

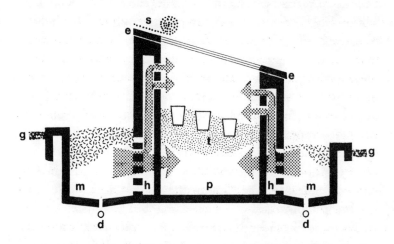

Cross-section of pineapple pit showing simple heating system

m = manure trenches   e = English lights
g = ground level   s = hessian screening
t = tan bark   p = evaporation pans
h = hollow walls   d = drainage

the honeycombed wall could reach as high as a hundred and twenty degrees if the fermentation wasn't controlled in the trenches. Indeed, in the early literature there were many unhappy tales of pits burning down after the manure burst into flames. Managing the temperature was an important job, and the heated glasshouses needed twenty-four-hour supervision to prevent mishaps. For this reason there was a 'squat' bothy, a small, simple bedroom, in the two-storey building above the thunderbox room, where the most junior of the qualified garden staff would sleep. He would wake every three hours to check the heat of the manure and, in later years, to stoke the boiler which replaced this technology. On the inside of the pit's hollow walls, perforated slate baffles broke the race of warm air and at the same time prevented vermin getting in and eating the pines. The pit was covered by thirteen glazed frames known as English lights, the glass cut in the traditional 'beaver-tail' style. Sections through the sides of the pit show that it was originally made of wood, but was probably bricked up around 1860 when a stoke hole (boiler house), containing a horseshoe or saddle boiler, was added to the back of the rear pit, which itself was then converted into the three-quarter-span melon and cucumber house that we see today.

In the middle of the nineteenth century the passion for growing pineapples died among the gentry and was taken up by the middle classes. Faster sailing times from the West Indies probably played a part, as pineapples could now be delivered fresh on the quaysides of most English ports, robbing them of much of their mystique. It is also true that a new passion was gripping the imagination of the gentry – orchids. All over the country, special glasshouses were being designed to cater for this new craze, so Heligan's pineapple pit was consigned to history, converted first into a melon pit and finally a simple cold frame. By the beginning of the First World War, no trace of its former use remained.

The productive area was the engine room of the garden. It was Peter Thoday who pointed out the irony that none of the great gardens in Britain celebrated the tradition of the working garden, preferring to emphasize the pleasure grounds and their associations with lords and ladies at leisure. However, from the supposedly humble walled gardens, those pleasure grounds were stocked with marvellous plants from around the world, propagated and nurtured, developed and hybridized to a perfection rarely seen in the wild. In the glasshouses, fruits and decorative plants were being produced in defiance of natural conditions and were admired by all who saw them. A majority of the garden staff worked here, yet their story was never told.

The working buildings which nestled together against the north- and east-facing walls of the western half of the Melon Garden had a charm of their own, but afforded little comfort to those who had to work there. Light was far too valuable to sacrifice for human comfort so their gloomy aspect afforded minimum daylight, supplemented, when absolutely necessary, by oil lamps hung from the rafters. By the time electricity arrived, the lights had already gone out in the Melon Garden. There were no fireplaces to keep the workers warm. Even though Cornwall is considerably milder than elsewhere in Britain, it is nonetheless one of the dampest counties, so it is easy to imagine the older members of staff suffering great discomfort from arthritic complaints. There was a small toolshed and next to it a potting shed, which, judging by the regular fixing holes in its rear wall, contained extensive racking for the clay pots in all their different sizes. Each size of pot had a number, indicating how many of them could be made from a single measure of clay. The 60s or 'Tom Thumbs' were the smallest, and the number 1s were the largest pots. In addition to the normal shape, there were also special pots for orchids, herbs and strawberries, with considerable regional variations of style. The full length of the wall in front of the windows was taken up with a potting bench, underneath which were several bays for storing various composting materials. Panels of zinc were often nailed to the surface of the rough timbered bench to prevent the gardeners getting splinters in their hands when potting up at speed.

Modern garden writers have a tendency to see the past through rose-tinted glasses. The only roses in the Melon Garden were there to provide a screen for the path through it that led up to the pleasure grounds. The image of ladies in gingham dresses bearing Sussex trugs filled to bursting with cut flowers and vegetables that have never seen earth or insects is romantic hokum. The reality was that these working parts of the garden stank to high heaven. At Heligan more than a dozen different types of manure were in regular use as a composting or heating medium, including what was euphemistically referred to as 'human night-soil' – the slops from the cesspit next to the two-storey building, in addition to all the material coming up from the Big House. In his growing notes for prize chrysanthemums, the head gardener ascribed his success to the use of 'seven-year-old goose shit'. One assumes that it wasn't the age of the goose he was talking about.

The other myth that needs dispelling is that the Victorians were dedicated to healthy, organic methods. In reality gardeners in the nineteenth century were spraying sulphur, cyanide, nicotina and strychnine on almost anything. The staff who worked in the glasshouses didn't have high hopes of enjoying their retirement, and not for nothing did the brass sprayers earn the monicker 'widow makers'.

The open-fronted equipment store, with its roof supported by two thick oak beams resting across granite uprights, was home to the large cherry-picking ladders and hand barrows, and its cobbled floor was used for storing newly prepared compost materials. This was lovingly relaid by John, using thousands of additional pebbles brought in from Portholland beach, courtesy of the neighbouring Caerhays estate.

The two-storey building had a fruit store above and a dark or forcing house below. This is where the spring bulbs would have been brought on for the Christmas table. It would have been a matter of pride for the head gardener to present a display vase made of moss and bursting with sweet-scented lily-of-the-valley to the lady of the house every Christmas Eve, and to provide daffodils and hyacinths for the festive season. The dark house would also have been used for forcing chicory, sea kale and rhubarb. Furthermore, the conditions there favoured the construction of a root clamp for storing vegetables over winter, in beds of sand. Upstairs, the fruit store would have been laid out from floor to ceiling with slatted racking for 'keepers', fruit which would last long after picking. One wall would have housed a special rack for grape bottles, looking uncannily like those used for taking urine samples. These were laid flat and contained water, and charcoal for filtering impurities. By inserting their stems into the necks of the bottles, bunches of grapes were kept fresh until they were required at the high table. The fruit-room windows would have been shuttered to preserve the constant light and temperature required for safe storage.

Next door, reached by a ladder, was the 'squat' or little bothy. A hurricane lamp and truckle bed, with a mattress made from long straw covered in sacking, were the only provisions for its occupant, who attended to the night time servicing of the garden. Underneath was the thunderbox room, used by all the garden staff and emptied each morning into the night-soil pit directly outside. The contents were covered by sprinklings of lime and ash to suppress the smell until, when full, the nasty job of emptying it was given to one of the juniors. Nothing was wasted. Once emptied, the walls of this pit would have been scraped with a sharp slate to collect the saltpetre that had formed there.

Our initial clearance and exploratory excavations complete, the salvaged pieces of timber and ironwork were photographed, measured and drawn. We began the process of restoration. From the first, John felt a special sympathy for the Melon Garden, making some of the younger volunteers uneasy with stories of his evening conversations with the ghost of one of the former head gardeners. It was only ever half a joke. He would claim that the restoration was being supervised; someone was watching over him. No short cuts would go unnoticed. I will never forget the day when John stood looking at the downpipe of the two-storey building, which emptied straight on to the ground, and said that if he had been the designer he would have built a cobbled drain to take the water away. When he dug down six inches under the loam there it was ... the cobbled run.

John understood that it was essential to restore the drainage system. As much as a third of all the restoration work at Heligan went on below ground, repairing the damage inflicted by the roots of the many mature, self-set trees which had grown straight through the culverts and drains. He began by bringing in a mini-digger to tease out these huge roots, and it became a familiar sight to see him on his faithful metal steed.

Once the drains were exposed and restored, the structural work above ground could begin. Sponsorship and grants provided most of the money and materials we needed. The original ironwork was salvaged from the glasshouses and taken to the engineers for shot blasting, red leading and repainting. The missing sections were reproduced by modern day engineering apprentices, using the surviving parts as a matrix. Tony Montague, a good friend of John's and a superb master joiner, began by rebuilding the timber frames of the melon and cucumber house and the pineapple pit, and later the cold frames in the western half of the garden, while John led the rest of the team. The working buildings around the walls of the Melon Garden had to be rebuilt from the foundations up, as the tree roots had weakened them structurally. Steve Nelson and Michael 'Tiggy' Duff volunteered to help and began by taking the stone buildings up from ground level. In the winter of 1992 the site looked like a scene from hell, yet slowly but surely the place was transformed. The stone walls of the two-storey building rose from the mud, deep pointed with lime mortar, eventually reaching the eaves. The roof joists went on, followed by the roof itself. We were determined, wherever possible, to use reclaimed materials. Much of our time was spent scouting around reclamation yards and old buildings. John also had his friends in the building trade on constant alert for useful bits of slate or cast iron guttering. During the winter of 1992, the goat-shed tearoom became a dry workplace for John to cut the beaver-tail glass for all the English lights in the cold frames.

When the Methodist Chapel at Nanpean was being demolished John put in a successful bid at auction to buy its pine floor. He was elated, but Steve and Tiggy were less than amused when told that the whole thing had to be denailed and removed inside twelve hours. However, the chapel was to provide all the timber for the floors of our working buildings and the benches in the potting shed and toolshed.

We had great difficulty finding a surface for the yard. Traditionally it would have been clinker, the hard ash from the boilers, but these we had not yet attempted to restore. After months of searching, we were put on to the Bodmin and Wenford Light Railway, where mountains of clinker from the boilers on their steam engines lay waiting for a purpose. Once this was laid, the yard felt complete; the builders and their debris were evacuated, and the noise stopped.

Satisfying as it is to see a structure restored, it remains essentially a still life, dead, until touched by the breath of function; and here, that meant gardeners and gardening. To see fresh earth double dug and enriched with copious amounts of manure lifted everyone's spirits. Using the detail gleaned from the metal detector research, Philip McMillan Browse had tracked down most of the fruit trees we needed, in small specialist nurseries in Britain and France. In early 1994 he set about planting all the espaliered and fan-trained trees at twelve-foot intervals along the curved south-facing wall, with the soft fruit, mainly gooseberries and red- and white currants, set between them. Blackcurrants were not in vogue, being grown in the orchards only for cordials. A collection of cordonned pears was planted along the west-facing wall, and old varieties of violets and strawberries were reintroduced to the cold frames.

We brought in tons of horse manure to begin teaching ourselves about manure heating. Even Dr Brent Elliot at the RHS Linley Library was nonplussed when we came looking for instructions on using manure heating for pineapple pits. His encyclopaedic knowledge led us to dozens of articles on simple hot beds, but nothing on pits. Most eighteenth- and nineteenth-century books on gardening were written by head gardeners. Brought up within the apprenticeship system, they must naturally have assumed that anything as basic as manure heating would be known to their readers. We spent months expensively failing before we started to get the hang of it. It was expensive because we didn't have any horses and it took about a hundred tons of manure to fill the trenches. We eventually had to buy it by the truckload from a racehorse stable in Devon. Our only consolation was that racehorse manure heats up faster. It is essential that the manure is both fresh and mixed with straw, to allow for the reaction between the oxygen in the straw and the uric acid that has soaked into it. The Victorians referred to manure as being ready to use when it was sweet, meaning that it had been rinsed and allowed to dry. Usually water was sprinkled over the manure once it was in the trenches to achieve this effect.

With the traditional manure heating system finally working, we still had a problem sourcing any of the eighteenth-century pineapple varieties. Philip had concluded that they were no longer available in the western world and resigned himself to failure. One wet February day our luck changed. In the Melon Garden I came upon a man soaked to the skin, looking very sorry for himself. We got into conversation and he volunteered that he was the director of the Government Agricultural Research Station in East London, near Durban in South Africa. They specialized in pineapples, and he offered to take a look in the gene bank on his return. Six weeks later a fax came through: he had two of each of the varieties we were seeking. Would we like his students to propagate one hundred of each? Was the Pope Catholic? In July 1994 I went to Heathrow airport and collected one hundred 'Jamaica Queens' and one hundred 'Cayennes'.

On arrival at Heligan the prognosis didn't look good. When we emptied the pineapple suckers out of their hessian sacks they were desiccated and brown; but the staff potted them up and lovingly nurtured them until the following spring, when they were ceremonially plunged into the tan bark bed prepared for them. The pineapple pit was steaming again, for the first time in more than a century.

By 1995 the Melon Garden was back to full production. There are now cucumbers dangling from the beams of the melon house and melons hanging in string nets, as of old. Pineapples are growing in the pineapple pit – though so far they have steadfastly refused to fruit. Over the last few years we have assembled an extensive collection of old tools, some of which is on display in the toolshed. There are small specialist hand tools such as fern-lifting trowels, daisy and dock extractors, various makes of brass sprayers, clippers and vermin traps. The large hand tools include turfing irons, trenching spades and long straw-cutters and a fine assortment of early wheeled seed drills and hoes. Next door the potting shed is back in action. Our gardeners have made it their own. The racks are filled with terracotta pots of all sizes, some generously donated and others begged and borrowed; the broken crocks are kept in bins for other purposes. Raffia for tying hangs from the wall and the compost bins smell warm and sweet, blending with the other distinctive odours of creosote, lime and damp to create that dark, rich scent so beloved of gardeners all over the world.

An enormous thirty-foot cherry-picking ladder, made from one tree split down the middle, hangs from the wall of the equipment store: too dangerous to use any more, yet too important to burn. Beetroots and black radishes lie on sacking upon the cobbled floor, ready for eating, and the hand barrows lean against the wall. Upstairs in the fruit store, hundreds of onions are drying and boxes of our treasured rare potatoes await chitting for next season's crops. The wall fruit is not yet cropping heavily enough for much storage to be needed but, in the dark house below, the root clamps brim with turnips, carrots, parsnips, celeriac and Jerusalem artichokes to feed us through the winter, and the forcing pots have provided us with scrumptious chicons of chicory, tender stems of rhubarb – and some rather dodgy sea kale. The smell of the moist earth inside them triggers a delicious memory ... of toad-hunting, I think.

Chapter 10

DECLINE

In August 1914, the Heligan estate was in its prime. It had been run with seamless continuity for more than twenty years. Although Jack Tremayne became squire only in 1901, he had returned home to Heligan in the early 1890s and his father had been happy for him to take over the reins. His first major work was to supervise the construction of the stone dam which created the third pond in the Jungle. This section of the valley provided a natural high-sided amphitheatre, with a relatively flat basin in which to create the 'Japanese' effects he was looking for. Local people brought up after the Second World War at Heligan Mill and in the cottages in the woods below the Jungle remember a number of slate bridges linking little islands in the stream leading into the third pond. Having been of an age to view the Jungle as a wonderful stage set in which to have adventures, they remember only that it was highly colourful and cannot recall the planting themes on the islands. The slate bridges were purloined some time after the war, to grace the floors and fireplaces of some of the cottages. In fairness, no one believed that the Jungle would ever be part of a garden again.

Jack had a great love of Italy and often took holidays there. He bought a group of peasant cottages on the Riviera to convert them into a villa, where he was to develop another superb garden. Here he would experiment with planting ideas, with a view to synthesizing them at Heligan. But before the First World War all his creative energies went into his Cornish home. As well as the Jungle, he created the alpine garden in the Ravine and the Italian Garden adjacent to the Melon Garden. The evocative picture of Jack sitting in his newly created Italian Garden, or 'Suntrap' as he called it, was taken in 1909. He looks out from the summerhouse over the rectangular pool, with the fountain playing in the foreground. The Mediterranean-style beds and the creeping herbs planted in the cracks between the paving stones leave no doubt as to where the inspiration came from. Early pictures of the Ravine give the same impression of Italian influence in its plantings and strongly resemble those taken in Jack's garden in Italy.

A fierce patriot, Jack tried to enlist in the army as soon as war with Germany was declared, only to be told that at the age of forty-five he was too old. When the war began it became obvious that there would be many casualties and Jack decided to turn Heligan into a convalescent home for officers. Nurses were employed and, while some of the key domestic staff remained to help him, the gardeners were reduced to a skeleton crew as each passing month drew them to the enlisting stations at Bodmin and St Austell. By 1916, the twenty-two outside staff were reduced to eight looking after the whole estate, and the only gardening of interest now was food production; the pleasure grounds would have to wait – and pay the price. At the start of the Great War, the Royal Navy's ageing fleet was mostly of timber construction and the Admiralty appealed for donations of oak. Jack had the great oaks in the eastern shelter belt felled and replaced with Monterey pines, which he thought would make a suitably fast-growing substitute.

New Orchard of Cornish apple varieties

Flower Garden

Jungle

Heligan House

Flora's Green

Vegetable Garden

Melon Garden

The productive gardens were designed to meet the demands of the Tremayne family in the big house. During the nineteenth century the garden staff worked with and defied the seasons to provide a constant and varied stream of fresh produce for their sustenance and delight.

Within the productive gardens
the mid-Victorian bee-bole
wall served a prime purpose –
pollination. Our apiarist returned
several traditional straw skeps to
these sheltered recesses.

The Melon Garden (opposite)
was identified early on as the
heart of the productive gardens
and its structural restoration
was undertaken in stages
until all the working buildings
were complete.

From left in distance (above): tool shed/potting shed, open-fronted equipment store and two-storey building with three cold frames in front. The melon house dominates the foreground with a manure trench separating it from the pineapple pit.

The melon house on discovery was a forlorn
sight, but within three years Gillian was
tending cucumbers and soon afterwards we
were harvesting melons.

The restoration of the pineapple pit was our biggest single challenge. Rebuilding it was one thing – raising old varieties by traditional methods was quite another.

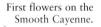

First flowers on the Smooth Cayenne.

On a private visit in June 1997 H.R.H. The Prince of Wales was enthralled by our progress.

The view through the northern gateway of the Melon Garden into the Vegetable Garden is transformed, between 1991 and 1996. One of the finest eating gardens (opposite) develops once more from childhood, 1994, to maturity, 1999.

Today the management of the productive gardens is as labour intensive as it ever was. The annual cycle of horticultural labours is still rewarded by the harvest. Clockwise, Mike gathers carrots and Tom delivers produce to the tearoom; Gillian bundles an armful of Swiss chard and Rachel (a student) picks from a wall of sweet peas.

Sweet dreams are made of this.

The cucurbit family at home.

Among the early patients was O.G.S. Crawford, a flying officer who would later become famous as the pioneer of aerial photography in archaeology. He wrote his first book on the subject while convalescing at Heligan.

The last patients left in 1919 and Jack renewed his visits to Italy, renting Heligan out from time to time. In the late 1920s he decided to set up permanent home in Italy, leasing Heligan to his friends the Williamsons. A wealthy New Zealand family, they maintained Heligan to a high 'Edwardian' standard until the start of the Second World War. While they were keen gardeners, the Williamsons concentrated their efforts in the immediate area around the house and in the large walled garden. Many of the photographs that helped us with the restoration were donated by Mrs Williamson's daughter, Tab Anstice. Everyone I have ever met who remembers this period in Heligan's history, male or female, has said that Mrs Williamson was the most beautiful woman they had ever seen.

One of the joys of the restoration has been its never-ending capacity to throw up surprises.

In the summer of 1993 Frederick Draycott drove all the way down from Keighley in Yorkshire in an old Morris Oxford. He was revisiting Heligan for the first time in more than sixty years. His father had been the head gardener around 1920–31. He filled us in on some of the detail of the years between the wars. The Melon Garden had been allowed to slip into dereliction during the First World War and afterwards no one had bothered to reclaim it. During his father's time, he remembered that extra cold frames had been built in front of the peach house in the Flower Garden to replace the loss of vegetable production in other, already derelict areas. Mr Draycott later wrote to us with more of his reminiscences:

The vine glasshouse 1918/30 was in full production. I spent hours in the winter watching Bill Cox de-bugging the vines, a long back-aching job, sat on a high ladder, day after day. He would be telling me tales of stoking up HMS Barham in the Battle of Jutland.

The only bothy in use I witnessed was by the 'boiler' compart-ment rear of the vinery. Grapes were grown each year, good ones … The number of permanent garden staff was small, but bolstered up with temporary staff, usually available through the twenties, as and when the gardening seasons came and went … everything was so different to the period before the War.

There were peacocks and there were friendly emus on the East Lawn who would frequently escape and come and pull at the lobes of one's ear. The emus also made great pals with Edward, the donkey, who earned his keep pulling the lawn mower prior to 1924 when a Denis 4 stroke motor mower arrived [and made him redundant] … Finally there were monkeys who amused visitors and staff with their antics … Heligan, like many other estates was very quiet, so much so one could hear from afar peacocks, hydraulic rams, turkeys, monkeys, oil engines, dynamo and circular saws, motor cars and mowing machines etc. … our fox terrier dog who kept guard at our house gate could hear Father's trap horse entering Lower Lodge gate on the Pentewan road, well over a mile away – and he would take off, to meet him coming home.

At the start of the Second World War, the Williamson family moved away and the house was filled first with inner city children and then with refugees. In 1939 Jack Tremayne, wanting to be at home in time of war, returned to live at the Stewardry on the estate. Commissioning an enormous painting of Il Duce and placing it prominently in the back of the removal truck, he was able to leave Italy with most of his possessions intact.

The Americans arrived to practise for D-Day on the beach

at Pentewan, and it was not until 1946 that the house reverted to the family. The historian A.L. Rowse, who lived on the
cliffs to the east of Pentewan, told me of venturing into the
Jungle with Jack in that same year. It was apparently much
overgrown by then and the lakes were filling with leaves, but
there were the most beautiful drifts of primulas everywhere.

After Jack's death in 1949 and the subsequent auction, the
Thomas family took up the tenancy and came to live at
Heligan. They tried to keep up the gardens, but the house
itself was in serious disrepair and needed a lot of money
spent on it. I had the good fortune to make the acquaintance
of Mrs Pat Thomas before she died in 1995, and from time
to time I still see her two daughters, Gill and Sue, who were
brought up at Heligan. Commander Thomas was keen on
camellias and rhododendrons and took copious notes on
their colours, names and locations. The family had a business
selling cut flowers to Covent Garden. Their head gardener,
Fred Varcoe, recalls that when they arrived at Heligan, the
bee-boles and the Melon Garden were lost, although the
main rides up to Flora's Green remained in good order. The
Jungle, barely penetrable and not much more than a swamp,
had become a favoured trysting place for courting couples
walking up through the woods from Mevagissey.

In 1970 Heligan House reverted to the estate and was
converted into flats. Lack of finance made it a slow process
and presented thieves with many opportunities; garden
ornaments, large plants and even the lead flashings from the
greenhouses and outbuildings were stripped. The mahogany
bookcases from the library were reputedly put on a bonfire
on the front lawn. In 1972 the Tremayne family advertised in
the RHS Journal that anyone wishing to help themselves to
plants should come to Heligan, as very soon the gardens
would be no more. I have met many who briefly considered

it, before deciding that the specimens were too large to move. Mike Nelhams, curator of Tresco Abbey Gardens, told me recently that they nearly invested in a lorry to take out all the tree ferns from Heligan – it makes your blood run cold. The gardens went into free fall.

One by one the new flats in Heligan House were sold off, the estate finally relinquishing its freehold in 1983. Storm damage and the encroaching overgrowth took the Jungle and the productive gardens, and the rides became narrower and narrower until by 1990 they too were impenetrable. The gardens immediately surrounding the Big House were of course maintained and Ivor Herring continued to salvage what he could from the dereliction beyond. The only other tenuous link with a glorious past was the series of small allotments established by several of the new residents in the Big House, within the wilderness of the Flower Garden.

Decline is hard to arrest; like rust it never sleeps. Once the Tremayne family accepted that they had no realistic chance of living at Heligan again, a fatalism set in. There was some sadness; Jack's nieces, Damaris and Penelope, had fond memories of family visits but they had never lived there, so its loss, while a matter of regret, wasn't a bereavement. Since Jack had departed for the Italian Riviera, the strong bond with the past had been broken.

John Willis, who invited me to meet him at Pentewan Sands after the 1990 hurricane, is Penelope's son and Jack's great-nephew. The trust set up for John and his sister Antonia took over responsibility for the gardens in 1989. It was a liability that would weigh heavily upon them. When John first took me to see his wilderness, something was stirring inside him. Perhaps it was a question of pride, a compulsion not to let his inheritance 'go gentle into that good night'. Whatever it was, John made the restoration possible, by persuading his trustees that all was not lost. Since then he has been a staunch supporter and a good friend to the project, which in turn has reaffirmed the ties that bind the Tremaynes to Heligan.

Chapter 11

THE CAST TODAY

The world is a much changed place since those heady days at the Big House, when the squire could afford to indulge his curiosity about the world beyond these shores and the ladies were ladies of leisure. In all but a few cases, the role of the English country house, with its well managed estate at the centre of a thriving but dependent community, has gone for ever. The squire and his family, with their privileges and social responsibilities, have been replaced by new owners who have, of necessity, a narrower focus. Most of the buildings on the Heligan estate have been sold off and there are over twenty flats in the house itself. Ironically, a number of staff involved in the garden project now live at the Big House.

A century ago, Heligan's twenty-two garden staff would all have lived locally, either in the cottages on and around the estate, or in the nearby villages of St Ewe and Mevagissey or the little hamlet of Pengrugla just outside the main gates. The rigid hierarchies of employment so typical of the Victorians, in which each man knew his place, were restricted to perhaps a hundred or so large estates where the apprenticeship system was firmly established. Smaller estates like Heligan would mostly have reaped the benefit of training given elsewhere. The lack of sufficient bothy accommodation to house apprentice under-gardeners, and a staff roll containing only local family names (precluding 'journeymen', travelling garden craftsmen), imply that the estate did not give many apprenticeships. The head gardener would have been a highly trained craftsman, who had risen through the ranks from under-gardener, journeyman gardener to foreman, gaining as wide a range of experience as possible before taking up a position as the top man. The staff roll at Heligan suggests that there were a couple of foremen (one for the productive gardens and the other for the pleasure grounds), perhaps six gardeners (a craftsman grade) and no more than two under-gardeners in apprenticeship. The rest would have been garden labourers with a fair grounding in horticulture, but with a capacity for wider estate maintenance tasks. Below them came the pot boys, probably young local lads with no higher ambition than to become garden labourers.

When we began the restoration in 1991, our manpower was limited. John Nelson, joined by Dave Burns whenever he was on shore leave, led teams of volunteers. Then there were the Noyce family, me, and Rob Poole whenever his zoo commitments permitted. Philip McMillan Browse offered horticultural advice, with Sue Pring contributing on the design side. We were all aware that the scale of the project demanded permanent staff as soon as possible.

Orlando Rutter, Rob Poole's friend, had won his spurs as a volunteer during the first days of clearance in the Melon Garden. In the middle of 1991, a grant from the Countryside Commission allowed us to appoint him as our first team leader. I found Orlando to be one of the most exuberant and enthusiastic people I have ever met. A wild-eyed, devil-may-care appearance, which so inspired his troops in the field, leading them on to ever greater challenges as the months went by, belied a caring and responsible man who was to lay the foundations of Heligan's training organization and set the tone for the subsequent development of our permanent workforce. When he and his girlfriend Julie Hopley left at the end of 1993, so that he could continue his academic career, they were sadly missed, and will forever remain part of the Heligan folklore.

It was Orlando, using his woodland management training qualifications, who first set up courses to train unemployed people at Heligan. In the midst of the recession there were many willing recruits, some of whom made the mistake of assuming that this would be a soft option, another of those schemes where the unemployed were treated like cannon fodder, then spat out once the course was over and their usefulness as cheap labour came to an end. Orlando was merciless in his demands. In return he offered real training, devoting many hours of his free time to bringing on the less able who were falling behind. The uncommitted hardly had a chance to pack their bags. Loyalty was the benchmark by which Orlando judged people, and he promised jobs to those who demonstrated it, putting us under increasing pressure to find the funds to pay for them. The first tier Orlando filled were the garden labourers.

One of the earliest arrivals was Kenneth Renowden, a man in his late thirties with some educational difficulties which had prevented him from ever having a proper job. He came to us on a placement via a training agency. He could barely speak and brought all his worldly possessions with him in three plastic bags for fear they would be stolen from his bedsit while he was at work – a habit he still can't shake off. His other phobia was safety. He would wear indescribable layers of clothing against the elements and on one occasion he donned a hard hat for weeding. We couldn't bear the thought of Kenneth's gloomy prospects when the placement ended, so Orlando nursed him through his basic exams and then he was taken on to the permanent staff. Kenneth was once overheard talking to some American tourists who had asked him how long he intended staying at Heligan. 'For ever if they'll have me,' was his reply. 'For ever is a long time,' said the American. 'Well, I' been waiting a long time,' replied Kenneth. He is known as the bramble king, because of the manic single-mindedness of his scorched earth policy towards the invaders. His straw hat and stubbly chops are reminiscent of Vincent Van Gogh, an impression not dispelled by his rather Delphic pronouncements. Just before Christmas 1991, Orlando and Rob prepared a team feast at Palm Cottage. We all felt a little emotional when Kenneth, after a small glass of Rob's infamous home brew, looked unbelievingly at the spread and announced that he had never had a Christmas dinner before.

Charles Fleming arrived by the same route. A wiry ex-printer in his fifties with hearing problems and a shock of white hair, he is one of the most hard-working men I have ever met. His horticultural limitations were far outweighed by his willingness to do anything asked of him, with a good humour that made everyone smile. Single-handedly he has double dug the borders of the Flower Garden. He is a stalwart of the tractor crew which collects manure from local farms and seaweed from Port Mellon cove after an easterly blow. His leisure interest is writing a diary of the restoration of Heligan, which he now publishes himself. A great favourite with visitors, he has cultivated a Kenneth Williams style of high camp which, when mixed with his deafness, can lead to bouts of hysteria. On one occasion we came upon a group of visitors with tears streaming down their faces. Apparently one of them had asked Charles whether a clump of flowers were Canterbury bells, and he had replied that he didn't know because he couldn't hear them.

Simon Lawday was another character who blossomed at Heligan. He is far and away the strongest man on site and also probably the gentlest; more often than not he sports a beatific smile as if he's just had a vision. In his early twenties, he was desperate to find a job and volunteered to work for eighteen months for nothing. A speech difficulty had affected his self-confidence, but from the moment he received his first pay cheque he became a changed man, gained his qualifications and is now regarded as one of the core members of the garden staff.

Orlando welded together a superb team, combining volunteers, trainees and new staff who had come from the ranks of trainees. This in itself gave each new intake the incentive to make an effort. He led the team through the project's major clearance phase, in which they tackled the Italian Garden, the main rides, the Ravine, the Vegetable Garden and the Melon Garden. They uncovered the ram pumps, replanted the bulk of the shelter belts and cleared most of the Jungle. He ended his career at Heligan in an unbelievable three-week blitz, with John Nelson and the team clearing a two-mile-long Georgian ride. If I had to choose one single memory of Orlando it would be the great daffodil planting in the autumn of 1992.

While the skies opened up, 40,000 bulbs arrived on a truck and the sacks were hastily unloaded into the goat shed tearoom, half filling it. For three weeks it rained stair rods. With each day that passed, more and more of Flora's Green disappeared under a sheet of water. Orlando and Julie would set out at dawn with the team in their cagoules and not return until dusk, soaked to the skin, covered in mud, but unbowed. They left Heligan a year later, in time to start the autumn term at Wye College in Kent. When they drove off in their bile-green East German Trabant, made of army surplus bandages held together with resin, it was the end of an era. It always struck me as humorous that a man so committed to environmental issues could drive such an amazingly noxious vehicle.

If Orlando could be said to have led the pioneering phase, Robin Leach, our first head gardener, was to lead the settlers into a new era. The project now needed someone with sound horticultural knowledge at the helm. Robin joined Heligan in September 1993 along with two other new faces: Rod Lean, a year-out student from Hadlow College, and Tom Petherick, who lived locally. Rod made himself instantly at home and, although not yet fully qualified, took responsibility for the pleasure grounds under Robin. Tom had come to see me and asked for a job for the autumn. His home was Porthpean House, overlooking St Austell Bay, where his mother Charlotte grew champion camellias. He had just returned from Kerala Province in India, where he had been working on a permaculture project, and welcomed the chance to spend some time with his family and to play his beloved cricket at weekends. His autumn job was to last for three years. Philip took him under his wing and, as the clearance and building teams moved out from one area after another, the two of them began developing the productive gardens. First they worked on the Melon Garden, then the Vegetable and Flower Gardens. Philip would create the planting schemes and source the materials, thereafter acting as Tom's mentor in the implementation of his plans.

Robin's first big job was to oversee the clearance of the Flower Garden. We had secured a grant from the Rural Development Commission for the restoration of the structures within its walls – the vinery and the citrus and peach houses – and for the banana house and the working buildings in their traditional location on the outside north-facing wall. This grant was augmented by one from the Countryside Commission, for the restoration of the paths, drains and cultivated areas of the Flower Garden. The rest of the resources we found from sponsorship. The main driving force behind this restoration was time. We had ten months in which to complete the work; if we overshot the end of the sponsoring organizations' financial year we would lose the grants.

That autumn John and I made the best investment of our lives. As insurance against bad weather we ordered a large polytunnel, to house the craftsmen constructing the frames for the glasshouses in the Flower Garden. A military operation got under way. All the structures were photographed, technically drawn and then dismantled. The main timbers were taken away for computer profiling and new ones would return from our sponsors, accurately cut, ready for hand finishing and painting. The metalwork was taken down and sent to the engineering apprentices who had helped us with the Melon Garden. Meanwhile the huge original 'cultivated' area was being cleared by Robin's team: the self-set trees were sawn down, the few remaining fruit trees were saved and heeled in elsewhere, and there were bonfires in every corner of the walled garden.

'Flower Garden' is in fact a misnomer. While it was used to grow flowers for cutting and its glasshouses overwintered the exotic pot plants that would later be exhibited in the public rooms of Heligan House, it remained very much part of the productive garden complex. Its warm and sheltered beds were the most protected in the garden, in which were grown the more tender and perennial vegetables, saladings and herbs. Its walls traditionally harboured a range of pears, cherries and apples. The glasshouses, although designed for particular crops (citrus, vines and peaches), were put to many and varied uses throughout their long history. This was the location of the exotic glasshouses full of 'curious and aromatic plants' described by that visiting antiquary in 1824.

The great wall was built around 1780 of brick imported from the Low Countries, brick being a scarce commodity in Cornwall. The glasshouses situated along the south-facing wall date from the 1840s. Furthest west on this wall is the tropical house, which was used for citrus, and adjacent to it stands a Paxtonian Fruit House in two sections. Historically this is perhaps the most important structure in the garden. It was designed by Sir Joseph Paxton, the head gardener of the Duke of Devonshire at Chatsworth House in Derbyshire. (This was the most innovative estate in Britain, but the contents of its great walled garden were unfortunately bulldozed in 1981 to make way for a caravan park.) Here the Duke allowed Paxton to experiment with all that the Industrial Revolution had to offer, in a quest to create the finest glasshouses in the world.

It was Paxton who went on to design the Crystal Palace in Hyde Park for the Great Exhibition of 1851. With an eye to its commercial prospects, Paxton linked up with Samuel Hereman to design a prefabricated modular glasshouse which could be transported around the country. Marketed to the public through the columns of the *Gardeners' Chronicle* under the banner 'Glasshouses for the Millions', it was aimed at the burgeoning middle classes in the new suburbs springing up around the industrial towns of the Midlands. It was designed to house the king of Victorian table fruit, the Muscat grape. By 1850 this was undoubtedly the most popular greenhouse in the world. Today there appears to be only one left: the one at Heligan.

Adjacent to the Paxtonian Fruit House was another range of glass – probably a stove house and a fig house. All that remain are the foundations, some wall scarring and a large, heavily fruiting fig. These structures were knocked down in 1860 to make way for the latest craze, a free-standing full span orchid house. By the time we arrived in 1990 this was listing under the weight of brambles and only the finial at its entrance was visible. The unheated peach house on the west-facing wall, built around 1880, completed the original collection of structures.

The greenhouses, though rotted out, were sufficiently complete for accurate templates to be made. The polytunnel team of master joiners Tony Montague and Tony Holmes and painters Norman Miller and his mate George went into action. Up went the peach house, then the Paxtonian Fruit House and the citrus house, with the glaziers following on behind. The maintenance of this range of glasshouses has become like that of the Forth Road Bridge, and the painters have remained as permanent staff. Lead paint would have been used in the past as its porous qualities enabled the wood to breathe, but current health and safety practices required a substitute, the quality of which is still to be tested.

John Nelson and Charles Fleming were completing the restoration of the drains. They linked up the culverts, fed by the downpipes of the glasshouses, with the small brick-lined pond in the middle of this garden, which was known as the Dipping Pool. This is where the pot boys would have dipped their buckets or watering cans to fill them. The pool collected all the freshwater run-off from the garden because the Georgians and Victorians believed passionately in the superiority of rainwater over tap water, as it was soft. The Dipping Pool had to be partially rebuilt after a huge operation to remove an overgrown Irish yew, whose roots had broken through the side of it. Originally intended as a formal, clipped specimen, it had bolted to over sixty feet high, shading a large part of the garden.

By the end of summer 1994, the glasshouses were finished and John had put in the paths. Tiggy Duff was working his way around the top of the four walls, removing self-seeded saplings and repairing as he went. Thereafter he started on the head gardener's office on the outside north-facing wall. Seeing the thin wisp of smoke drifting up from the chimney once more was a wonderful moment for us all. Tiggy boiled a kettle hanging from the original hook in the fireplace and made a pot of tea to celebrate its return to use. It felt really good – but the tea tasted awful. The bothy next door and the banana house were finished soon afterwards. We were going to meet the deadline.

When Peter Thoday challenged us to 'play the whole opera', I don't think any of us can honestly say that we understood the full implications of our decision. Most of the great gardens of England have reverted to a 'maintenance only' policy, with very little active horticulture taking place, let alone restoration work. The reason is simple – anything other than this is extremely labour intensive, especially in productive areas, and therefore prohibitively expensive. More than that, a 'maintained' garden can accommodate a fairly flat management structure, allowing the head gardener to work alongside the staff without sacrificing control. An established garden, however large, can be managed by one person with an ability to delegate. Seasonally based operations are mostly a matter of routine, around which all other considerations can be centred. However, the myriad demands of a large scale garden restoration, with its targets often driven by funding availability rather than good horticultural practice, can make a head gardener's job a nightmare. As if these pressures were not enough, Robin's active commitment and obvious talent for horticultural training stretched him to his limits. Mastering the mountains of health and safety legislation, training certification and general administrative paperwork brought Robin, a gardener by birth, to his knees. Before Christmas 1994, as an act of mercy, we relieved him of his responsibilities and in the New Year re-employed him to co-ordinate our training programme. The whole staff rallied to support a popular and long-suffering colleague, very much a victim of circumstance.

Winter has never been a time for gardens to take on additional staff, and our critical financial situation meant redeploying the existing team on the basis of what we had learned. Earlier that year Philip McMillan Browse had finally done the decent thing and begun working four mornings a week as Heligan's horticultural director, specifically to supervise the reconstruction of the productive gardens. His relationship with Tom Petherick was already yielding remarkable results. As a temporary measure we asked him to widen his brief to include the pleasure grounds.

Annabel Turner's reputation had travelled to Cornwall in advance of her arrival from Wisley, where she had been their prize student. In September 1994 she replaced Rod Lean, who had returned to Hadlow to finish his studies, despite all our blandishments. We had rented a desirable but barely habitable farmhouse on the Caerhays estate to house her and several new year-out students. We were somewhat taken aback when she turned up with her boyfriend, Jim Walton, and it soon became evident that he had no plans to move on. However, instead of simply hanging around as a distraction, he did some serious work on the house and then volunteered to come and help in the gardens. He was prepared to do anything just to be with her, and would soon prove himself indispensable.

Annabel began by working in the pleasure grounds as a qualified gardener under Robin. She had an air of calm authority and a fiery temper. Having demonstrated both knowledge and reliability over her first few months with us, Philip suggested, on Robin's redeployment, that she should lead the pleasure ground team. She and Tom got along well and shared the everyday garden responsibilities between them. Over the next few months the workforce naturally divided into two – for the pleasure grounds and the productive gardens. Subsequently we split off a third team, to be led by Mike Helliwell, who had turned up as a ridiculously over-qualified volunteer. We decided to employ him, once funds allowed, in the spring of 1995. His area of responsibility was to be the Jungle and the woodlands beyond.

Philip, John Nelson and I were aware that this arrangement of three joint head gardeners, with no full time top person, was a little unusual but it saw us through that season. We concentrated our resources on the productive gardens, whose future development had already been meticulously planned by Philip and Tom. The other areas were more problematic. We had already commissioned a restoration planting plan for the pleasure grounds but its completion was much delayed, which left Annabel and Mike in a holding position. The plans were finally on the table in the summer of 1996. By this time the structural restoration of the Northern Gardens was almost complete and we realized that the moment had come to make important decisions about the future of Heligan. It was obvious that if we wanted to pursue horticultural ambitions, we would need to find a world-class gardener. If we did not, the magic of the gardens would be sold as pastiche, and the horticulture would soon be no more than a case of the emperor's new clothes. We searched for six months before finally securing the services of Tim Miles. His ambitions match our own and we are now looking forward to an exciting future with Tim as director/curator of the gardens, supervising both the plants and the people of Heligan.

As a new chapter opens in which horticulture is a priority once more, it is strange to note that the staffing structure now mirrors almost perfectly that which was in place at Heligan at the turn of the century, when the gardens were at their finest. The structure is in place to carry on where Jack Tremayne left off.

In the Flower Garden, the first year's display of flowers for cutting reached its peak in July 1995. It took the breath away. Our visitors were captivated by it. The view through the doorway which had first excited my imagination was transformed to the vision we had all carried with us on our journey. Row upon row of sweet peas, clarkia, love-in-the-mist, cornflowers, poppies, cosmea, scabious and lilies delighted the eye. Originally the flowers would have been destined for the public rooms of the Big House.

How fitting, then, that in August Annabel Turner and Jim Walton, by then resident in one of the flats there, should have their wedding day adorned with floral displays of which any head gardener would have been proud. As the horse and carriage drove up from Gorran Church to Flora's Green, the whole community at Heligan turned out to celebrate. Sweet-scented and romantic, it was above all a living tribute to those who first worked here, from those who now hold the keys.

Chapter 12

IN THE SHADOWS

The garden restoration was going on at a breathless pace, as if our lives depended on it and slowing down might break the spell. The visitors flooded in and their encouragement spurred us on. They were as pleased and delighted as we were by what they found at Heligan, and we enjoyed the sensation of having a gallery of 'friends' to play to, who would come on a regular basis to check our progress.

It would be less than honest to say that relationships always ran smoothly. The sheer exhaustion of many of the team, combined with the often unrealistic demands put on them, created tensions that inevitably surfaced from time to time. However, by the end of 1993 the pressure was beginning to tell and the general feeling of tetchiness was replaced by a black mood that seemed to permeate all aspects of our lives. I can't say precisely when it dawned on us that something might be deeply wrong. I suppose it crept up and caught us by surprise, but I can clearly remember a moment when, taking stock, it was obvious that both our working relationships and our private lives were close to breaking point.

The backcloth to it all was a series of unexplained incidents. Each individual episode could have been laughed off as a single event, but the steady accumulation of bizarre happenings started to sow seeds of doubt in our healthy scepticism. I neither believed nor disbelieved in ghosts or other paranormal phenomena. Like most people, in my youth I had read horror stories and the novels of Denis Wheatley, with their lurid accounts of the 'other' world, but I had read them as entertainment. My grandparents' home, Hartford Hall, where I had often stayed as a child, was built on the ruins of a monastery. Older members of the family sometimes claimed to have seen and felt things that they couldn't explain. My granny, who talked to her 'ghosts' as if they were old friends, told me once that she had seen the figure of a monk over my crib. However, in the absence of any personal experience, I had taken it all with a pinch of salt.

I began to view these things more seriously after talking to a friend of mine, a down-to-earth character with whom I played football for the Clapham Casuals. As a reporter for the South London Press he had volunteered for an assignment at a house in Nightingale Lane, whose residents the council had been asked to rehouse on the grounds that a poltergeist was making their lives a misery. He had been looking forward to debunking the story and was to spend two nights in the house as a guest of the family. Apparently the first night and most of the following day had passed quietly. Convinced it was a hoax, he had made up his mind to leave, when suddenly all the lights and electrical appliances went on and off and ornaments flew across the room, smashing against the walls. A frenzied knocking came from the bedroom above, and he had raced up the stairs to investigate it. On entering, all was silent. Then, in his words, the air went thick with pressure and a low moaning sound built swiftly to a roaring crescendo. The double bed in the middle of the room burst into flames. The heat was intense, but to his amazement the flames died as suddenly as they had come. The bed showed no visible sign of the conflagration and, doubting his senses, he peeled back the bedclothes. The undersheet had been burned to carbon, yet nothing else was even singed. His skin crawling, he made his excuses and left. He was clearly shaken, and all of us Sunday footballers who heard the story were in no doubt of its truth.

It was to be some years before I was confronted by these issues again. Every big house has ghost stories attached to it. That comes with the territory. Soon after my arrival at Heligan I began to hear stories of the Grey Lady, who was said to be regularly seen walking away from the house. In fact, that part of the ride between the house and the shelter belt woodlands is often referred to on old maps as Grey Lady's Walk. An old lady in Mevagissey, who in her youth had been a servant in the house, told me that she had once seen the apparition and followed it into the trees, where it had disappeared into a mist. A number of residents in the house also told me of doors opening and closing for no reason and of echoing footsteps. This all sounded like run-of-the-mill stuff to me.

Then I heard a strange tale. In 1978 an Australian plumber, working on the flat conversions in Heligan House, had discovered the overgrown Melon Garden and decided to camp there. He had collected wood to build a fire inside the ruins of the two-storey building but try as he might, he could not light it. Suddenly, the whole wood pile burst into flames which shot high into the night sky. They formed the shape of a cross and died immediately, leaving only a pile of cold ash. Terrified, he ran to the house, explained what had happened, packed his bags, left and was never seen again. I would have enjoyed the story more if I hadn't been struck by the parallels with the haunting on Nightingale Lane. Otherwise, it bore the classic features of the hair-raising nonsense that had been all the rage when I was in my late teens.

After the gardens opened to the public, I began to receive a steady stream of letters and phone calls from visitors, relating extraordinary stories of their experiences in the gardens, some of which were incapable of rational explanation. If it had ended there, I suppose I might have been pleased and intrigued. After all, ghosts have a romantic appeal that would lend a nice touch of Gothick to the gentle melancholia already present in the gardens. However, it didn't end there.

Some experiences had possible explanations, in that they concerned visitors coming to terms with a recent bereavement. Individuals were often convinced they had been accompanied by their late husbands or wives, for hours on end, as they lost themselves in the atmosphere of the gardens. Others described feelings of being 'not alone' in the rockery and Wishing Well area, and several claimed to have seen someone walking through the wall of the Crystal Grotto. When a group of psychics visited, some said they could tell me the names of the tragic couple who used to meet secretly in the Grotto, while others, with knowing looks, asserted that there were dark humours abroad.

While John continued to ascribe the accuracy of his detailing to those regular evening chats with the old head gardener in the Melon Garden, among the garden staff there was an atmosphere of embarrassed unease. They would joke about the spooks in the garden, but it was obvious that none of them felt comfortable locking up the gardens alone at night. Several admitted to having heard what they thought were footsteps in the fruit store. Philip McMillan Browse complained that his seeds were moved, with no explanation, out of locked rooms. One evening a couple stopped me and told me that the previous week, alone in the Melon Garden, they had gone into the dark house, under the fruit store, where all the forcing pots were laid out in a row. They described watching, transfixed, as the pot lids were lifted one by one, as if someone was going down the line checking on the crops inside. After the last lid was replaced, they claimed to have heard a deep sigh and then no more.

By December, although the restoration of the Flower Garden was proceeding as planned, the sense that we were not in control of our own destinies grew even stronger. I have never felt out of my depth in that way before. One day John returned from the valley to the south of the Jungle, where he had been collecting ferns to pot on in preparation for an exhibition. He was ashen and shaking. He had been out on the Tump, surrounded by ancient beeches and holly trees. His dog Fly, her hackles raised, had refused to go on with him. He had found this peculiar but, after an unsuc-cessful attempt at coaxing her, he had proceeded alone. Suddenly the hairs on the back of his neck stood up and he became aware of something . . . Out of the ground, in broad daylight, an enormous black shape had appeared and slowly drifted out of the trees to nothingness. It is hard to know what to say at times like this.

A couple of weeks later there was a dreadful tragedy. Steve Nelson lost his wife in a fire at their house in Mevagissey. John and his wife Lyn took Steve and their two grand-children into their home and the wider community suffered with them.

'It is perhaps fortunate that the church is such a comfortable institution. Were people truly to understand the nature of the battle between good and evil, they would be terrified. The church, not just our church or indeed our religion, is at war and I cannot, with my hand on my heart, say that we are winning.' The vicar paused and looked at me thoughtfully. 'Are you a believer?' I shrugged, ill at ease. 'You see, as long as good and evil are represented as being on opposite sides in a fairy story, they have only the power of allegory, and mean different things to different people. Unless you have seen or felt evil yourself, you can have no idea of its strength. It is only then that you realize it is an absolute.'

The vicar came to Heligan at my request. I had called him in as a last resort. I felt awkward explaining that while I didn't necessarily believe in ghosts, I had a problem with them. Far from treating me like a crank, he took the matter seriously and reassured me that I had contacted the right person.

We walked to the various locations where 'activity' had been at its highest, ending up at the Tump. He grew more intense here, sensing something qualitatively different. He said he felt that this place had an association with evil. In the leaves under the ancient beech and holly trees were bits of wood stuck in the ground which, when their alignment was cleared, formed a satanic pentacle. This was fairly fresh and must have been made by people coming here in secret for many years. We started back on the long walk to the garden entrance and the vicar confided that he would need to take special advice from the Bishop. Our talk then turned to ghosts and paranormal 'possessions' of which he had had personal experience. He discussed a disturbing case of a girl brought to him at the church. Her friends had carried her in and she had writhed on the floor, speaking in strange languages with a voice that changed from an unbelievably bass growl to a high-pitched whine. He had been frightened but had prayed over her for several hours, until her body went limp, bathed in sweat. When she came round, she had no memory of how she had arrived at the church or of what had happened. Such occurrences were rare, said the vicar, and all but one case involved a young woman. The same was true of the 'poltergeists' he had seen. He was a rational man and believed that the explanations were probably locked somewhere in the human brain. In time, science would reveal the secrets of these extraordinary events. Ghosts were a different matter. He spoke of them in fairly conventional terms, as spirits in need of release after missing the boat to the afterlife. He had visited a surprising number of houses, blessing them and seeking to lift whatever burden was shadowing the atmosphere. He also talked of ghosts in relation to places of great sadness or tragedy. Some human beings and many animals were acutely sensitive to their presence. But exorcism, said the vicar, was extremely rare. This was a weapon used against the forces of evil. Some of his fellow priests had known cases ... His voice trailed away and he obviously didn't want to continue the conversation.

A few days later he returned, having taken advice. We were to visit all the identified locations and enact a ceremony in each place. The exorcisms consisted of the solemn incantation of a number of holy words followed by the generous sprinkling of holy water. The early spring sun was shining and the birds were singing their hearts out, which added a surreal quality to the proceedings – that and the fact that the vicar was travelling incognito, in a jacket and trousers, like any other visitor. We stopped at the Mount, the Crystal Grotto and the Wishing Well, followed by the two-storey building in the Melon Garden, before finally winding our way down to the Tump. After the last incantation, I gave the vicar a tour of the gardens, thanked him and said goodbye. At the time, John Nelson, my wife Candy and I were the only people aware of his visit. With a new season around the corner we hoped that the garden would now be at peace with itself. All we could do was to wait.

Chapter 13

OUT UNDER THE SPOTLIGHT

The apparent resolution of these extraordinary experiences brought a quiet relief amongst those who knew. Within days, independent reports confirmed a lighter, happier atmosphere in the gardens, a lifting of that sense of foreboding, and specifically the absence of that oppressive haunting sadness which had held certain areas in its grip. The exorcism was one of the few events in the garden that passed unnoticed by the world at large; indeed, our endeavours to secure its privacy not only achieved that end, but, as people spontaneously noticed a difference, secured the proof of its effectiveness.

From the very beginning we had involved our visitors in our plans and learned to live our everyday lives in the public eye. The spotlight had its own dynamic, which would not allow us to get away with anything less than whatever we had promised. To keep faith with our public, we put ourselves under the constant pressure of achieving new goals. Commitments made, we were forced to fulfil them. The restoration was closely scrutinized; a visible error or omission soon drew comments and had to be rectified. Best of all was the comradeship which developed out of the gruelling challenges we undertook. In our relationships with sponsors, funders, neighbours, friends and even the media, there was a sense that everyone out there, for whatever reason, was urging us on, willing us to succeed.

The first project in which we experienced this constant sense of being observed was the mammoth task we set ourselves of reclaiming the Vegetable Garden. This 1.8 acre 'plot' was originally enclosed by a clipped laurel hedge to east and west and a thuja and Lawson's cypress hedge to the north, with its southern end bordered by the walls of the Melon Garden. The 1839 tithe map shows it divided into four by a cruciform path system lined with fruit trees, and it was serviced by a pair of cart tracks on its east and west boundaries.

On our arrival the Vegetable Garden was completely over-grown, recolonized by a mountain of bramble and self-seeded trees. The clipped laurel boundary hedges had encroached thirty metres from either side. The coniferous northern hedge now dominated the skyline, shading out not only the Vegetable Garden but also the ornamental avenue of Chusan palms planted alongside it. This defined the separation between the productive gardens and the pleasure grounds on the southern edge of Flora's Green. Three beautiful old apple trees were all that remained of those that had once lined the central path through the Vegetable Garden. Their perfect shape and association with a time when the garden was still in full production made the possibility of their loss hard even to contemplate. Torn between logic and sentiment, John and I were worried that acting in haste might lead to a long repentance at the garden's expense. For months we hesitated. Both Philip McMillan Browse and Peter Thoday were frustrated by our reluctance to clear out the remains of the conifer hedge and all the overgrowth. They believed that the restoration would be unacceptably compromised without a fresh start.

And so, in the end, the offensive began on Boxing Day, 1992. All our families, with assorted house guests and friends, arrived to work off Christmas dinner. We had already decided to keep the gardens open to the public throughout the winter, since we would in any case continue to work there. The hive of activity on site provided unique festive entertainment. The chainsaws whined into action like angry wasps. As the evergreen giants fell, they were dismembered by a group of adults who passed the pieces to an army of children, who in turn were feeding the massive bonfires which had sprung up right across the Vegetable Garden. By nightfall the site looked as if it had been attacked by a swarm of locusts. The large trunks were removed by digger to our storage area in the shelter belt, after which the digger returned to extract the roots. John set the challenge to complete the first phase of clearance within the week, before Orlando and his team returned from their holidays. With his son Steve, Tiggy Duff and Dave Burns, he worked from sun-up to sundown to meet the target. By New Year's Day the Vegetable Garden was completely cleared, except for a scenic copse of mature willows and the old apple trees. They had uncovered the gateposts of the original entrance and some of the drain runs, and they had traced the course of the cruciform path.

A tractor came to plough the ground, after which the team walked the area, painstakingly removing all the bits of roots and brash that remained in the soil. John then feverishly set about the replacement of the path network, borrowing his beloved mini-digger to scoop out the footings and prepare the ground for laying water pipes and ducting down through its entire length. Thereafter, mountains of hardcore were laid and rolled on to the paths. Earlier we had found some of the iron arches that had lined the main path through the Vegetable Garden and we now persuaded our engineer friends to replicate them for us. Tiggy and John set the arches at measured intervals down the new path and welded them together. It was a miraculous transformation. Shape and form had been restored in but a few months, and a sense of order prevailed.

When John and I first met, he was musing about taking early retirement, promising himself an allotment. He loved growing vegetables. Now he would have his chance. He and Dave had to work like maniacs through to the early spring of 1993, turning the south-western square of the Vegetable Garden to a fine tilth so that John could plant his seeds in time for the coming season. He took a proprietorial pride in seeing his giant allotment develop through its first year.

Philip kept chipping away at us. He was adamant. Romance be damned: the apple trees were in poor condition and gave too much shade. Their abundant blossoming in 1993 was to be their final show. Reluctantly, John and I gave in. The day the apple trees were cut down was a sad one for us. We felt as if we were betraying old friends. Our relief was almost tangible when the stumps revealed the presence of a fungus which would have killed them sooner rather than later. Philip's opinion was vindicated.

Philip would soon be able to start composing the Heligan opera. First we had to construct the stage. The rear wall of the Melon Garden was cleaned up to carry trained fruit, and the laurel hedges were severely cut back to give more space. The replacement thuja hedge along the northern boundary was already doing well. Philip is an active crusader for the preservation of Cornish apples, which, up until a few years ago, were heading for extinction.

In the autumn of 1993 (top) John and I consider the next challenge – the wreckage of the Flower Garden. Eighteen months later the neat, regimental rows of spring shoots belie the back-breaking labours which transformed it.

The vinery in the Flower Garden – before and after. A picture is worth
a thousand words.

The fruits of our labours.

This mural view from the
southern wall of the
Flower Garden shows the
peach house (delicious
fruit, inset) and the
adjacent, restored Sundial
Garden. There is an
original, interlinking
gateway about half way
along the wall.

'Heyday', from the archives, followed by dereliction and despair. In 1996 Damaris Tremayne re-opened the restored Sundial Garden and the public passed through the gateway from the Flower Garden …

... where the old wisteria thrives (opposite). The original handkerchief tree (*Davidia involucrata*) (close-up, top right) holds court over a colourful revival last staged more than forty years ago. Pat Thomas at the sundial c.1950 (top left).

Out in the wider estate, heavier work proceeds ... 'Their big tufty hooves
moved with a delicacy that belied their size.'

The restoration of the Lost Valley was conceived to enable native species to thrive and traditional woodland management skills such as charcoal burning to be undertaken again in harmony with the environment. John masterminded the restoration of the lakes and the creation of the island for the wibbly-wobbly tree. He protects his achievement with a fierce pride.

The oldest oak in Old Wood shades one of the Georgian Gallops – silent witness to the rise and fall of one of the most mysterious estates in England.

So naturally he decided to reintroduce them to Heligan. Even though elsewhere in England pears would have been chosen to train along the arches, Philip selected some appropriate varieties of traditional apples which stood a better chance of coping with the Cornish climate.

By the time of Tom Petherick's arrival in the autumn of 1993, John's first season in his allotment had illustrated the enormity of the challenge ahead, and Philip had already prepared a planting plan based on a classic four-year crop rotation. This was designed to break the cycles of many soil-borne diseases and to nurture the soil. The path network divided the Vegetable Garden into four segments, each of which would eventually be at a different stage in the rotation (thus each of the four squares would represent one year of the rotation). The ground was prepared with many days of double digging and the addition of large amounts of seaweed and manure, brought in to enrich and aerate the soil.

We started by selecting crops on the basis of flavour rather than strict period correctness. Any head gardener worth his salt would not knowingly have chosen a variety with inferior flavour, once a better one became available. Whereas today we look forward to the arrival of gardening catalogues, in the nineteenth century the early autumn visits of the seed merchants were awaited with eager anticipation. The case for growing some modern varieties could be made on the grounds that experimentation, comparison and change reflected the spirit of the head gardener, if not the period which the restoration sought to evoke. However, in the end Philip's researches turned up such a wide range of vegetables and fruits that almost all the varieties we now grow are traditional ones, first introduced before 1905.

With the demands for standardization brought about by Britain's membership of the European Union, many superb varieties are now no longer available because they lack homogeneity. While this may serve the narrow interests of present day food producers, it hugely impoverishes the palette of flavours available to us. The commercial sale of many vegetable varieties is now forbidden by law, and so they can be obtained only through seed exchange between collectors. Philip secured plants and seeds from a wide range of sources. Substantial numbers came from the Henry Doubleday Research Association at Ryton, near Coventry, which has a marvellous collection dedicated to the preservation of heritage vegetables. Many of our potatoes were obtained from Mrs Maclean of Crieff in Perthshire, Scotland, whose husband had maintained the best collection of potato varieties outside Peru. After his death she had kept the flag flying. Philip was sent half a dozen of several varieties he wanted, and planted them to bulk up for seed. Now, several years later, we have many hundred-foot rows of potatoes. Each variety has its own attributes. Belle de Fontenay, Pink Fir Apple and Ratte are excellent for salads, Golden Wonder (a traditional variety!) is perfect for frying – and making crisps, and Edzell Blue is renowned for its decorative colouring. We have also grown May Queen and Ninetyfold, which are original Cornish early potatoes.

The most striking characteristic of many of the older varieties of fruit and vegetable is their distinctive flavour. Modern varieties often have the blandness of texture and flavour of baby food, in comparison with the strength of their traditional counterparts. Older varieties of potatoes, turnips, swedes, beetroot, beans of all sorts and, of course, strawberries surprised and delighted us and we discovered black radishes as powerful as chillis. An unusual crop, no longer commercially available, is the drying bean, grown for storage and for use in soups and stews. Philip acquired the

Lazy Wife variety, evocatively named on the dubious grounds that its leaves fall off so that the beans are easy to see and to harvest. Sampling them all became a highly pleasurable occupation, mostly. One supplier sold us a collection of fifteen distinctively flavoured varieties of rhubarb. Having loathed rhubarb at school, I was not surprised to discover that I disliked them all. Our staff ate very well, having access to the pick of the crops rather than the leftovers, as would have been the norm for their Victorian counterparts. However, each newly discovered delicacy from the past made us despair at the price we pay for living in an age of convenience.

Philip's plan included setting out the perennial vegetables and fruits in their permanent beds, beginning with the asparagus. Its hundred-foot run was dug to two spades' depth, part infilled with sand, planted, mounded up and then covered in seaweed.

One of the most exciting sights in horticulture is a wide expanse of well tended vegetable garden. In the summer that vision now includes the espaliered apples and grandiflora varieties of sweet pea, trained along the arches down the central path. Beside them grow wide bands of sweet william and, later in the season, rows of pompom chrysanthemum. Beyond, on both sides, climbing beans on their frames create a textured wall which acts as a windbreak for other crops. The strikingly coloured flowers of the Czar and Painted Lady beans add to the impression of exuberance. Row upon row of military straight lines, with mixtures of height and foliage, present a cornucopia of riches to drive a gourmet mad. All the craftsman gardener's tricks of the trade are on display: from companion planting and Tom's special applications of comfrey tea to discourage pests, to the heat management of the rhubarb, sea kale and chicory forcing pots, to the enrichment of the dark fertile earth, the most valuable asset we have, coloured by Victorian soot to absorb the heat of the early spring sun to best advantage.

Almost everyone is captivated by the Vegetable Garden. Whether this is on account of a romantic memory of Beatrix Potter tales or an interest in the crops themselves, doesn't matter. Tom Petherick and his colleagues Mike Rundle, Gillian Cartwright and Paul Haywood soon became the first and last port of call for many of our visitors. These members of staff were willing to spend hours each week both offering and receiving advice. If there had been a conspicuous loss, owing to an unexpected frost or an unwelcome overnight scavenger, these minor disasters invariably evoked a public response, if not always a sympathetic one. Soon a regular mutual fan club developed, with visitors coming to buy our fresh, organic vegetables and often donating plants from their own collections for Tom and Philip to try. This rapport is an essential theme at Heligan today.

In September 1996 Tom finally took his leave, having made a huge contribution to the restoration of the productive gardens over the first three years of renewed intensive cultivation. He has taken up a wonderful offer to mastermind the restoration of another overgrown vegetable garden, owned by friends. Fortunately for us, and most unexpectedly, we found someone to take his place immediately. He is the former head gardener of Enys. Historically one of the most important gardens in Cornwall, Enys has been obliged to cease active horticulture this year. Richard Dee has a wealth of experience and mouth-watering ambitions to build on Tom's achievements. We await next year in the productive gardens with eager anticipation.

The special relationship we have with our visitors is nowhere better illustrated than by the popularity of our

'Friends' organization. When we first opened, Rob Poole recommended issuing season tickets. No commitment was originally intended on our part other than to provide free admission during normal opening hours until the end of that year. We had no idea whether the project would outlast the first winter. When Peter Thoday made his initial visit to Heligan in July 1992 and agreed to give a public address in the evening, we decided to mail our Friends, about fifty of them, to see if they might swell the audience. The response was overwhelming. The following year we offered member-ship, and tickets valid for a full twelve-month period. By the end of 1993 there were 300 Friends of Heligan. Even at a great distance, people were kept in touch with our progress by substantial newsletters, which Candy compiled and mailed out three times a year. Fans in Germany, New Zealand and the States continue to renew their membership year after year, as do local people, who simply can't keep away. This constant desire to return and find out what's new explains in part the attraction of Heligan. We hold several functions for the Friends every year, sometimes offering privileged access to newly discovered areas or simply invit-ing them to enjoy the garden at its best, after the crowds have gone home. By 1996 we had 1,200 Friends, many of whom have chosen to become lifetime members. In the same year we were paid the compliment of being invited to twin with the Friends of the Royal Botanic Gardens, Kew. This is an association we treasure, as Kew is the foremost horticultural establishment in the world and Heligan is the first private garden to be honoured in this way.

In terms of timing and pace, the development of the Vegetable Garden corresponded to that of our office admin-istration; throughout 1992 we pretty much ignored both.

Rob stashed receipts and invoices in the passenger footwell of his zoo van, and for a while the rest of us turned a blind eye. It was obvious things would have to change.

In the autumn of 1992 we built another wooden shed which was divided into two rooms. One was for our friends from the British Trust for Conservation Volunteers, who set up their Cornwall HQ with us; the other was for us. But it was not until the following season that we employed our first administrative member of staff, a part-time book-keeper. The demand on the tearoom was such that Lyn Nelson had to run it as a separate operation, so we also took on two people to share the ticket office duties. Both of them remain with us today, although they now play different roles.

Before the restoration began, Frances Matta, a stylish cosmopolitan lady of Cornish origins, had bought herself a flat at Heligan House to use as a bolthole from London. Some time later she gave up her job and decided to move back to Cornwall. Our first meeting with her was inauspicious: her little terriers were attacked outside Palm Cottage by Rob's cat and the subsequent exchange of views introduced us to the richness of her language. Peace was restored, however, and thereafter she was often to be found in her winter furs enjoying the views from the newly restored Northern Summerhouse. We discovered that she was bored and, when we suggested that she might like to help run the ticket office for a wage that was an insult, she agreed. She truly loves Heligan and has been known to have champagne breakfasts in the Italian Garden. She regularly welcomes the dawn from the bottom of the Jungle with her two little dogs. Fran went on to develop our plant sales area, where she remains to this day.

The other stalwart is Colin Howlett, who also joined us in 1993, under unusual circumstances. I went to the Llawnroc, looking for someone else to share the ticket office rota with Fran. Colin was at the bar. I knew him to be a keen naturalist, who had moved to Gorran Haven after taking early retirement from a position as marketing director of a major international electronics company. He took me aback by suggesting himself for the job. He didn't need the money but would welcome the involvement. In his first year he also gave the occasional guided tour around the garden and as winter approached he offered to help us in the office. This was to change both Heligan and Colin.

He set about establishing order from chaos and insisted on instituting policies he considered vital in any organization. These included health and safety management and first aid, personnel functions and properly planned marketing. The autumn of 1993 was to set the course for Heligan's future success. Colin and I developed a database of all the garden clubs, Women's Institutes, coach operators and hotels in the West Country. This has built up over the last few seasons to include international interests and Heligan can now boast one of the most extensive garden databases. Every autumn we circulate every individual or organization on our list with an update of what is going on at Heligan. Colin consolidates this mail-out by attending all the major travel shows in London and Birmingham.

The first plank of our marketing ethos is that we do not want Heligan to become a typical tourist site. We want to offer a destination that we ourselves would wish to visit. We concentrate primarily on Cornwall. Every week throughout the winter Colin and I visit clubs and associations, giving talks and slide shows about the garden restoration. Outside professionals have commented that this seems to be a massive waste of labour, as we sometimes address only a handful of people in remote corners of the county. We argue that our strength lies in intimacy. There is no better advertisement than a recommendation from your neighbours. Most visitors to Cornwall, we feel, should come into contact with someone who has enjoyed the gardens. Between us, Colin and I have given hundreds of talks across the South West over the last three years. If we were to lose regular and, more importantly, personal contact with people we would destroy the very thing that makes Heligan special. Affordability of access is essential too. A garden that celebrates the skills of ordinary men and women must be within the budget of ordinary people, and we are determined that Heligan will always remain so.

In April 1994 John and I had the excitement of flying out by helicopter to the Island Hotel on Tresco, for the press launch of the 'Five Great Gardens of Cornwall'. It was the first time either of us had visited the Scillies and it was a mesmerizingly clear blue day. It felt like the start of something good. Representatives from Trebah, Trewithen, Probus, Heligan and the Abbey Gardens on Tresco had established a joint marketing initiative, compiling a colour leaflet to celebrate these wonderful Cornish gardens, without any hint of competition between them. This was to be distributed throughout the West Country and would give us a voice in speaking up for garden interests generally. We were delighted when in 1995 the National Trust joined us in our mutual advertising venture, giving us an even more powerful platform. In truth the 'Five Great Gardens of Cornwall' wouldn't have been successful if the people involved didn't enjoy each other's company. We co-operate on the construction and manning of exhibition stands for the Royal Cornwall Show and the Cornwall Garden Society Flower Show, as well as for trade fairs upcountry. Our stands are famous for having music and plenty of refreshments. If you can't enjoy yourself, why do it?

Long-term success can only be sustained by playing a role in the wider community. Jim Walton, who had arrived unexpectedly with Annabel in late 1994, soon discovered his natural vocation and assisted us in setting up the Heligan Gardens Charitable Trust. Through this he channelled his unstoppable energy into development of the educational arm of the project. He was building on foundations laid by Orlando Rutter, who had a special gift for making environ-mental issues come alive for schoolchildren. Who can forget whole classes of blindfolded infants tagging one behind the other around the gardens, touching, smelling, tasting, hugging and finally pretending to be trees? Or the group of Cubs navigating their way through the Jungle, using nothing but a mirror tile to reflect a route between the tree tops? Jim's arrival marked an escalation of our involvement with primary and secondary schools and colleges across Cornwall. Working closely with teachers, he developed educational strands that were woven into the National Curriculum. 'The Victorians', for instance, was a topic to which Heligan was ideally suited. Herds of schoolchildren visit us throughout the year and we have come greatly to value our special relationship with them. They keep alive a sense of wonder which serves to remind us all of why we are still here.

The relationship we have with the media is crucial to the success of the gardens. We have long cultivated our friends in the press, making sure that we had a regular stream of inter-esting material to give them. Heligan has had many stories covered in the local papers, on subjects ranging from the discovery of the ram pumps to the relocation of a swarm of bees by our resident apiarist, when they were discovered at the top of a huge, dead Monterey pine that was about to be felled. The national press was more tempted by stories such as the return of the pineapples to the only original manure-heated pineapple pit in Britain.

I remember our excitement at the first story that appeared about us in a national newspaper. Under the byline 'From west coast rock to rhododendron blues', on November 23, 1991, Anna Pavord of the *Independent* chronicled the discovery of Heligan, while giving a tongue-in-cheek nod to my past career in the music business. Since then, Heligan has been the subject of dozens of media stories, both in Britain and, more recently, on the continent and in America. We have enjoyed such good relations with the press that now they often come hunting, without any encouragement from us.

While publicity keeps the name of the garden in the public arena, it can lead to some funny moments. BBC Radio 4 wanted to broadcast a strand of their travel programme *Out and About* from Heligan. Impressed on their recce by the erudition of my fourteen-year-old son Alex, they asked us whether he could appear on the programme. Alex was delighted and gleefully made plans to spend the appearance fees. When he discovered there was no such thing on offer he went AWOL. Jim searched the parish for him and dragged him back to the gardens, making a bet with him that he wouldn't manage to bring up their favourite subject of football during the interview. Alex promptly became charm personified, escorting the radio crew around the Jungle and knowledgeably naming all the rhododendrons for them. To our horror – but to the great entertainment of many listeners – he introduced the world to the hitherto unknown joys of *Rhododendrons forestii, jason leeii, steve stonei*, and *mark crossleyii*, all of them members of his beloved Nottingham

Forest football team. The hoax was broadcast in its entirety to the listening millions.

We also worked up an April fool's joke with BBC Radio Cornwall, which backfired on us. The gist of the story concerned the discovery, in the top lake of the Jungle at Heligan, of a water lily thought to have died out more than a hundred years ago. This lily was unique. It had clover-leaf fins on its roots, enabling it to swim around the lake to catch the sun. It was discovered in the Andes, by Hoechl, a Czech plant hunter working for a German count from Bad Homburg. Later the count sent out another expedition, to secure the rest of the lilies and gain him a monopoly. Tragedy struck. The heating system in his conservatories failed during the big freeze of 1881, destroying almost all his plants. Only three lilies survived, to be won in an epic game of cards by a John Tremayne, on his Grand Tour. And so the lilies found their way to Heligan ... The only problem was that so many people found the idea plausible that they turned up to look for them. We were particularly worried that thieves, thinking the story true, might break in and steal what few species we actually had.

The BBC *Gardeners' World* programme of 1991 put us in the television spotlight for the first time. Thereafter Heligan featured in many magazine programmes on all the networks. The first full-scale documentary about the restoration of the Lost Gardens of Heligan, commissioned by Westcountry Television in 1993, charted the restoration from the beginning until the spring of 1994, taking priceless footage of the resurrection of the glasshouses in the Flower Garden. After regional screening the documentary, presented and produced by Trish Williamson, went on to be broadcast on Channel 4 on several occasions, and brought us to the attention of a much wider audience. It was also dubbed for a much smaller group – the Cornish speakers, whose language is almost as user friendly as my native Dutch.

Heligan has been remarkably lucky in its media coverage, and we are aware of the danger of believing your own press. We were thrilled for it to be described, by George Plumptre in *The Times* of October 23, 1993, as 'the garden restoration of the century'. It was flattering and gave massive encouragement to the team. However, the fascination of the garden world lies in the uniqueness of every great garden. Comparison between the work at Heligan and that of, say, Stowe, Biddulph Grange or Painshill is meaningless. Each has its own merits. Similarly the accolades from consumer magazines such as *Gardening Which?* ('our most recommended garden') and the *Good Garden Guide 1996* ('Outstanding Gardener of the Year') are a pat on the back, not an absolute. I felt like a fraud accepting the *Country Life* 'Gardener of the Year 1995' award. Friends roared with good-natured laughter at this Johnny-come-lately, with little or no dirt under his fingernails, receiving such a commendation. In reality an award such as that is simply a recognition of the hard work done by the whole team at Heligan. Our story has captured the imagination and people feel kindly disposed towards us – no more, no less. But it would be false modesty to deny that we are all immensely proud of it.

Chapter 14

LIGHTS, CAMERA, ACTION

In spring 1993, John Nelson and I had been to London to receive from David Bellamy a Shell Best of Better Britain Award. The function was held in the Institute of Engineers, near the Houses of Parliament. Wearing suits for the first time in three years, we almost laughed out loud when David Bellamy strolled out on stage in clothes of the sort we had just discarded in a left-luggage locker at Paddington. This was the first award won by the gardens and it proved to the first generation of staff – Orlando's clearance team – that the outside world recognized the quality of their efforts; it justified the gamble many of them had taken in joining us at Heligan. Other awards and consumer star ratings have followed with pleasing regularity, each one offering encouragement to successive members of the garden team. However, while recognition from afar was always welcome, the intrusive eye of a television camera was personal, and another matter altogether. John Nelson, Philip and I had batted for the *Gardeners' World* crew in 1991, but the West-country documentary, commissioned in 1993, involved the whole of our team. There was a little unease, perhaps engendered by bashfulness, but most of the staff took to the spotlight like ducks to water. Andy Warhol would have approved.

We were still basking in the afterglow of the first transmission of the Westcountry documentary, when I was approached by two people who wanted to discuss making an altogether different kind of film about the garden. Coming so quickly on the heels of the other project, I was surprised at the strength of their commitment. I knew enough about television to suspect that they would find it difficult to persuade any commissioning editor to fund a second programme on a subject covered so recently.

I underestimated their determination. Frances Berrigan and Rosemary Forgan were both respected television producers, whose production companies, Bamboo and Cicada, already had distinguished track records in making serious documentaries. They were planning an in-depth series about a year in the life of Heligan, seen through the eyes of those who worked there, and exploring the similarities and differences between its past and present-day communities – a human story. Together we worked up a basic proposal, incorporating the two big projects scheduled for the following year, 1995/96. These – the restoration of the Sundial Garden and the Lost Valley – would provide the dramatic impact of 'before and after', against the background of the seasonal ebb and flow of a working garden. The proposal was presented to Channel 4. After months of negotiation, hopes were dashed with the departure of the commissioning editor. Traditionally, a new incumbent would be unlikely to pursue proposals championed by a predecessor. We were lucky. The parents of the new Channel 4 editor, Sylvia Hine, were Friends of Heligan, and before long the news broke that we were to be the subject of a six-part documentary.

The garden staff greeted the announcement with the sort of enthusiasm normally reserved for a trip to the dentist. A camera crew, virtually living on site for twelve months, was going to expose them, warts and all. The example of the Royal Opera House when observed in this way was hardly encouraging. We couldn't expect the crew to make an anodyne promotional film about us. The holding power of six programmes would have to be sustained by human interest, as much as by the spectacular changes being wrought in the garden restoration. Concern turned to alarm when we discovered that two of the joint production company's most recent programmes were *The Fishing Party* and *The Club*, both award-winners, closely observed and merciless exposés of, respectively, a yahoos' fishing trip to Scotland and the running of a golf club. Neither programme could have been made without the trusting complicity of its victims.

We went ahead with trepidation. The freelance director, Vivianne Howard, took complete control of the project. She was a remarkable young woman of great warmth and intelligence, whose friendliness belied an iron will to get things right. She admitted to ignorance about gardening and horticulture in general, but her voracious appetite for knowledge matched the diligence of her research, and her commitment to capturing Heligan in the round won the sort of acceptance usually only accorded family members. Our one reservation concerned Vivianne's wardrobe, which made Vivien Westwood's look conservative.

For the twelve months from September 1995 we lived cheek by jowl with the TV crew of Vivianne, Pete the soundman and Chris the cameraman. The six programmes would cover different topics: One, the historical background, which was my baby; Two and Three, the productive gardens and the work of Philip and Tom's team; Four, the restoration of the Sundial Garden featuring Annabel and John Nelson; Five, the Jungle, exploring Mike Helliwell's domain, and Six, a blow-by-blow account of John's Herculean restoration of the Lost Valley.

Filming a television programme is mind-numbingly boring. The constant repetition of actions to catch them from all angles is necessary, ironically enough, to give the appearance of spontaneity. Sod's law guarantees a stream of interruptions, whether from natural causes such as bad light and rain, from intrusive noise made by curious visitors, aircraft or chainsaw operators or, most commonly, from the human frailties of getting tongue-tied, having fits of uncontrollable giggles, forgetfulness or being clumsy. Each day would start with a shooting schedule and usually end with a shooting scheduled. Time was our enemy and the seasons marched on, totally unforgiving. This was as true for the filming itself as for the completion of the planned restoration work in the Sundial Garden and the Lost Valley. The programmes had to be filmed side by side, one day often producing footage for two or three different episodes, which meant that the cameras and heavy recording equipment had to be carted up and down the length of the gardens during staff crib time (tea breaks). Viv accumulated a mind-boggling quantity and seemingly random collection of scenes, which would be unscrambled only when the filming itself was over. Nevertheless, confident that our director knew what she was after, we generally kept our tempers and, whether by luck or good judgement, managed to meet the final deadlines. To our surprise, we felt quite bereft when the crew eventually departed.

The Sundial Garden is an enclosed, half-walled garden, sandwiched between the southern wall of the Flower Garden and the outbuildings which abut Heligan House. A very fine herbaceous border used to run its entire length.

The brick wall of the Flower Garden had provided a warm backdrop for the display. A facing border fringed the side of Palm Cottage, our HQ in the early years. By the time we arrived this area had lost its distinctive features and initially we treated it as little more than a thoroughfare to the treasures beyond. It was overgrown, though not impenetrable, and its centre had been colonized by a number of small oaks. The southern border was occupied by a few old ornamental shrubs and specimen trees, of such size that any future restoration would have to take account of the shade they created. The Sundial Garden's one remaining asset was, at its eastern end, a superb pocket handkerchief tree (*Davidia involucrata*), whose lovely and unusual flowers were much admired.

In 1994 Stewart Harding introduced us to Toby Musgrave, a garden historian, who had just completed his doctorate and was looking for some practical experience of a restoration. He joined us initially as a volunteer, before graduating to his first commission – the development of a restoration plan for the Sundial Garden. Once the productive gardens were returned to cultivation, we set our hearts on restoring this one herbaceous border. It was the final frontier of the Northern Gardens. Cornwall is not much noted for herbaceous plantings, but we were hopeful we could restore this as an additional attraction to hold the public interest right through until the final days of each year.

In the depths of an endlessly wet winter, and after an initial round of metal detection for old plant tags produced nothing at all, Toby retreated to the archive. The earliest evidence of the Sundial Garden is in an article by W. Roberts in the *Gardeners' Chronicle* of December 19, 1896: 'Mrs Tremayne's Garden. This is a very charming enclosure, of about a quarter of an acre, filled with all kinds of old-fashioned flowers, which produce a gay succession from January to December ... and more approaches my own ideal of what an old English flower garden ought to be like than anything I have seen.'

What an incentive, to re-open the Sundial Garden exactly one hundred years after these lines were written. Toby carried out as much archival research as he could, but most of the nineteenth-century papers had been lost. This left the *Gardeners' Chronicle* article, the first and second edition Ordnance Survey Maps (1881 and 1907 respectively) at 1:2500 scale; a few photographs, including the aerial shot dated 1950; and a sketch found in the RIBA Library by George Kitchin, showing alterations to the southern gateway into the Flower Garden and dated October 1920.

The photographic evidence – all we really had to go on – was inconclusive. Whilst one picture clearly showed a double border, separated by a gravel path, which ran from the gateway of the Flower Garden up to the pocket handkerchief tree, the others illustrated a single south-facing herbaceous border running beside the Flower Garden wall, with a lawn separating it from a north-facing mixed shrub border adjacent to Palm Cottage. The Ordnance Survey maps confirmed that the borders had evolved through the years from 1881.

We drew up a design brief with Toby. We wanted a herbaceous border once more to run the length of the Flower Garden wall, a beautiful lawn with a sundial at its centre and a north facing border of shrubs, herbaceous plants and bulbs. To avoid damage from visitors' feet and for ease of maintenance access, we would replace the box hedges and gravel path with a two-foot-wide brick edging around all the borders.

Gertrude Jekyll-inspired borders are now back in fashion, but we preferred to mirror something of the adventurous spirit of the nineteenth-century Tremaynes, and took as our inspiration an early Victorian herbaceous border, such as that found at Arley Hall in Cheshire which dates from 1846. Toby drew up a plant list based on contemporary catalogues and consulted with Isabelle van Groeningen, an expert in the field. Philip McMillan Browse's contribution was to narrow the selection down to those plants that could cope with Cornwall's moister and milder climate, before presenting a palette of appropriate plants and plant combinations for us to choose from. Chris Gardner, a garden designer and contemporary of Toby's from university, was invited to come up with a new design within our chosen historical framework.

So much for the plan. Chris Gardner presented us with a finished design and now we had to make it real. We started in October 1995, with the biggest muster of staff in Heligan's history and the television cameras there to record the transformation. The whole team gathered for the assault. The oaks were sawn down, chainsawed into little pieces and carted away on the tractor and trailer. The area was strimmed off and the mini-digger, with John once more at the helm, came in to extract the roots. The following day the tractor returned, equipped with ripping machinery to break up the ground. Then the team hand-sifted the roots, stones and other rubbish. John meticulously marked out the oval-shaped path, using pegs and strings. When it was 'eye sweet', it was dug out. The weather for once was on our side and the team laboured solidly to complete the paths before the winter rain turned the ground to an unworkable bog. Ahead of schedule, before Christmas the borders were double dug and enriched with lashings of manure. After that, the team had to wait until March before they could begin planting the Sundial Garden.

Annabel started to organize her team. She had spent most

of the winter securing the delivery of Chris's huge shopping list of plants. The film crew were delighted to be back in action and their presence added to our sense of renewed purpose. Carefully, the gardeners transposed the planting scheme from paper plan on to bare earth, describing the shape of each planting group with a sprinkling of sand. Despite the weather prospects, they went ahead and planted.

Final preparations were made for the sowing of the lawn. Every pebble was removed. Then the ground was poked, stroked, raked and generally cherished until John and Philip pronounced it adequate. Even then the unseasonal cold persuaded us to wait until May before seeding it. Normally in Cornwall we would have expected perhaps five to seven days of frost a year, but our weather station readings confirmed more than seventy days at or below zero degrees from November 1995 to March 1996.

Now all we could do was wait and watch the grass grow. The film crew had set a plank on top of the Flower Garden wall, under the pocket handkerchief tree, as a fixed position from which to record the emergence of the Sundial Garden. The grass grew, the plants thrived. The film crew demanded an 'after' shot that didn't include the builders' rubble in the middle distance. In a fit of zeal John bestrode his digger like a colossus, blitzed the debris, levelled the ground and removed some large, intrusive *Rhododendron ponticum*. Horror of horrors, under the ponticum was a cluster of small gravestones. It was a pets' graveyard. These Victorian gravestones were removed for safekeeping while the ground was dug over, uncovering an unusual range of animal and bird bones, including an emu's. In an oversight we forgot to note the exact location of each, so 'Rover, we miss you so much' is now unfortunately probably on top of 'Tiddles the Cat', but it can't be helped.

★

There was to be a ceremonial opening of the Sundial Garden in July. The Friends' newsletter had included an invitation to attend the centenary celebration, and Candy had received two hundred acceptances. Damaris Tremayne had kindly agreed to do the honours, with John and Katharine Willis in attendance. Six years had passed since our first, rather tense meeting with Damaris at the White Hart Hotel. Through the intervening years of the restoration, she had gradually softened her stance towards us as she became comfortable with the way in which it retained the integrity of her uncle Jack's vision. By the time of the Sundial Garden's re-opening, we were able simply to enjoy the gardens together.

As the big day grew closer, we became anxious about completing the final detail in time. The residents of Heligan House had generously voted to return part of the original sundial base to the gardens, on permanent loan. In 1978 it had been removed to become an ornament beside the house. However, we were not only missing its original plinth but also an actual sundial for the top. My friend Mark Stocker located a first-class stonemason in Bath, who would carve the plinth and set a sundial for us so that it would keep accurate time. The stonemason, who apparently enjoyed much royal patronage, brought us various pieces of stone from which to make a choice. The clear favourite was the Portland, which, once weathered, would make a good match with what we had. It was ordered, rough sculpted in Bath and fine cut in situ at Heligan. Work was completed on the afternoon of the ceremony, in front of the cameras. The sundial itself had been found after our desperate plea went out on Radio Cornwall earlier that week. At the eleventh hour, a beautiful and expensive, early nineteenth-century brass sundial was delivered to the stonemason and fixed into place. All that remained was to fill two old Italianate urns with cascades of fuchsia and foliage, and pray.

Damaris arrived, once again with film-star timing, in front of a crowd that filled the Flower Garden with anticipation. After making a joke about the need to cut the ribbon twice in case the camera crew missed it the first time, she snipped it and declared the Sundial Garden open. She beamed all evening. Copious amounts of Pimm's were drunk in celebration and everyone strolled admiringly around the newly opened garden, in Indian file. Annabel and Jim, recently departed so that Jim could pursue a career in teaching, had made a special trip all the way from Manchester, and Toby and Chris had returned from upcountry just for the occasion. Viv asked them for their responses to the completed project and we retired, altogether in fine mood, to the Italian Garden for a picnic which lasted until dusk fell.

The Sundial Garden had looked lovely that evening, although to be honest the beauty was in the eye of the beholder. The jury was still out on several issues. Because some of the more unusual plants hadn't yet been delivered, the main border had an impressionistic feel to it. You needed to look at it through narrowed eyes to get the effect. The brick edging had a hint of suburbia, which we hoped would disappear with age. The plants should creep across it, softening its lines. The new seats, too, were loud in immature surroundings. Perhaps it was their clean whiteness which drew the eye, or maybe their proportions or location were wrong ... Only the sundial was cast in stone. The lawn was as smooth as a billiard table, as intended, but it gave the sundial the appearance of leaning into the wind, as it sat bolt upright against the slope of the grass – good time-keeping taking precedence over aesthetics. A subtle planting would soon cure that.

★

In September Viv finished filming with a lantern-lit shoot in the Jungle and returned to London, where she was to spend four months in an editing suite, wading through hundreds of reels of film, selecting bits from each, to weave the story of Heligan into a shape to satisfy friend and stranger alike. For the past eighteen months she has lived and breathed Heligan and, as I grapple with my own words for this book, I wonder at the enormity of her task. The clarity of vision an outsider might have been able to bring to the task was soon coloured by a deeper understanding of the gentle rhythms of each passing season, in a tradition largely unchanged over centuries and seduced by a spirit of place whose plangent theme runs through everything.

Chapter 15

PLATFORM FOR
A VOICE

The restoration of the Sundial Garden proceeded from an almost blank canvas, its structure blurred by continuous evolution over more than a hundred years. We have now successfully re-established a herbaceous border there, incorporating only nineteenth-century varieties; but the absence of any physical constraint encouraged us to consider, at the design stage, its modern-day usage – and the overall result has not fully satisfied our expectations. There is further thinking to do. Gardening is a dynamic process and the Sundial Garden will inevitably undergo continual fine tuning. It was ever thus. Maybe the pressure of meeting filming deadlines forced us to act in haste, but we were in any case, I believe, less well equipped to create a new blueprint than to restore a previously successful design. In every other area of the garden, the bones we had uncovered determined the shape of the reconstruction and set the mood.

It was bound to happen some time. We had been lulled into a false sense of security by the generous media coverage which the restoration of Heligan was receiving. The praise, in truth, diverted our attention from some of the philosophical issues affecting the nature of garden restoration. We believed that the pursuit of a romantic ideal, which had, after all, seduced us into a commitment in the first place, was enough. It was not until the spring of 1994 and a visit by Mary Keen, a respected garden designer and writer, that we were forced to examine carefully the ethos of our work. She pointed out that some of our 'restoration' work was, in fact, recreation. Indeed, as compromises have been made – the Ravine has been adapted from an alpine garden to a fernery (which we justified on the grounds of aesthetics, and historical precedent elsewhere), and plants have been introduced into some areas of the pleasure grounds which post-date the garden's decline – a purist might even quibble with the term 'recreation'. We argued that the garden we wished to see should retain the romance of its 'lostness'. We saw no need to reproduce what had originally been intended, when we felt that those intentions had been much improved upon by nature. Besides, the garden had evolved over a long period, absorbing the disparate influences which had captured the imaginations of succeeding generations of the Tremayne family. As a result Heligan has a highly individual if slightly eccentric feel to it, like the bric-à-brac collection on a favourite aunt's mantelpiece. Each object has a story to tell; none is valuable in itself, save as a reminder of happy memories and times gone by, but collectively they have the most precious attribute of all – a feeling of intimacy, of a unique identity. If we had slavishly restored every part of the garden to the period of its original design, we would have ended up with a series of unconnected period pieces, with no cultural glue to hold them together.

Mary Keen humorously pointed out in her article in *Perspectives* (June 1994): 'That quality of "unexpectedness" which Heligan now displays, and which was such a vital ingredient of the picturesque landscape, was satirised by the writer Thomas Love Peacock in *Headlong Hall* (1816). "Pray Sir," says Mr Milestone, "by what name do you distinguish this character of Unexpectedness, when a person walks round the grounds a second time?".' That, of course, is the problem. In answer, I would say that the picturesque influence on Heligan has, with the passage of time, been tempered in the service of a romantic atmosphere; the very effect they sought to create artificially in the first place – art imitating nature imitating art.

We have pursued two distinct restoration philosophies at Heligan. One governs the productive gardens and the other the pleasure grounds, although both remain harnessed to that indefinable quality, 'spirit of place'. The productive gardens needed to be faithfully restored to a working condition and managed in the traditional manner, if one was to tell the story of the men and women whose skills powered the engine room of the estate. Taking account of the long period in which they were in full production, we have restored their original functions to all the working buildings and glasshouses, with the exception of the boiler rooms (the boilers promise a challenge for the future), and have selected only crops introduced before 1905. It is widely recognized that here Heligan has made an important contribution to social and horticultural history. The pleasure grounds are different. Protecting the integrity of Heligan's designed landscape is vital, as is the preservation of its special 'lost' atmosphere. The skill is in harnessing the atmosphere to the needs of good horticulture. At the end of 1996 we are just setting out on this phase of the restoration.

Some garden historians seem to insist on purity as if some overriding aesthetic depended on it. Walking out of your own home to enjoy your own garden is a completely different activity from visiting someone else's garden, to admire its design or whatever. The first is an extension of domesticity, while the second invites an intellectual approach. Were an architectural historian to visit a family home to see an historic drawing room, for instance, and find it full of the normal clutter of family life – photographs, children's drawings etc. – its appearance might well not satisfy the intellect, yet as a home it would be unbeatable, and as a home it was designed.

Another issue which concerns garden historians is whether a restoration should take into account 'spirit of place'. This is not a reference to the subjective intuition of the garden restorer, but to a clear understanding of the ambitions of those who created the gardens, which they, for whatever reason, were unable to implement fully.

When we began work at Heligan we were conscious of our responsibility to the gardens so, when the restoration plan was drawn up, we made a commitment to pursue the strategy enshrined within it. One of the key aspects related to the Jungle, which had been identified as an important early Cornish valley garden. Our advisers recommended that we preserve it as such and effect only a narrow range of plant introductions, sympathetic to the mid- to late nineteenth century. Initially we were quite happy with this suggestion, but things changed when we discovered the stone dam, built at the end of the nineteenth century. In a recent discussion with Penelope Willis, Jack's niece, I discovered that he had often talked of his ambition to create as wild and natural a jungle garden as he could. He was an avid purchaser of the newest introductions and liked to exploit the possibilities of exotic floral and foliage plantings to the full, both in Italy and at Heligan. When I heard this I felt that to maintain a garden that is 'important' but limited in scope, when one could explore the full plant palette to create what Jack wanted to achieve, would be depressing in the extreme, besides being a poor tribute to a man of vision and artistic ambition. I further warmed to Jack when I was told that he believed that the gardens looked better slightly overgrown and 'secret' than when they were manicured. If the last owner-in-occupation would have approved of our work, that is good enough for me. As a result we have decided to let our new curator, Tim Miles, off the leash and, while acknowledging that Jack's only reservation concerned the use of inappropriately loud hybrids, we will allow him to develop the wildness of the Jungle to its full potential.

When we restored the walled gardens at Heligan, we used mostly reclaimed building materials, except where they were impossible to find; for instance we used some new, hand-made bricks in the wall of the pineapple pit, which we subsequently aged with yoghurt and manure. But our quest to retain the romantic mood at Heligan stopped short of compromising the original functions of the working gardens. There is a famous restoration currently underway, where the mossy bricks of the cold frames were taken down one by one and then used in the rebuilding. The idea was to retain the 'romantic' feel of the frame yard. The frame yard never was romantic, except in its dereliction. Any head gardener seeing moss on the bricks of his cold frames would have lambasted his gardeners for poor husbandry.

The greatest excitement in the restoration at Heligan has been to see function revived in its buildings and beds. Seeing peaches in the peach house, vines in the vinery, the vegetable garden generating barrowfuls of luscious produce and the potting shed a hive of activity again is an indescribable thrill. The gardens are the backcloth for a living community once more. Without the garden staff, the sense of purpose they bring to their work and the life they instil into the working buildings, Heligan would be mere history in aspic. It is this connectedness of place and purpose, form and function – of people enjoying going about their business but with time to share their pleasure and commitment with others – that has found a resonance in our visitors. That is the quality which has captivated their interest ... and which provokes them to return.

The labour-intensive nature of the project, which began with volunteers and grew to employ a paid workforce of more than fifty people, is now financed by gate money. I am often asked why Heligan should have become so popular, and popular not least among garden professionals, who might have been expected to be suspicious of its success. I believe the reason to be that we celebrate the best traditions of horticulture, and hold the profession in the highest respect. The last thirty years have seen a continuous undermining of the status of gardening, to the extent that the best and brightest students are actively discouraged from entering a profession now seen as synonymous with low pay and poor prospects. It is sadly ironic that the resurgence of interest in gardening and garden visiting corresponds to the nadir in the professional standing of horticulture. Heligan is horticulturally active, that is to say, here we have people visibly engaged in all practical aspects of gardening. Some of the major heritage institutions have a policy of gardening behind closed doors, as if gardens should look good by divine providence. Without more encouragement of horticultural professions, there is a real risk of a skills shortage developing which would have a catastrophic effect on the management of our great gardens. By allowing the public to come into contact with those who maintain, develop and care for their gardens, the profession will win back the respect it deserves.

Heligan has been enormously lucky in that it was able to benefit from circumstances which were not generally considered fortunate. The hurricane of January 1990 forced the Countryside Commission to extend the sphere for its grant funding into the West Country, thus enabling Heligan to obtain substantial financial support for its clearance operations, and subsequently, as the scope for these grants grew wider, for its structural restoration. Heligan became the largest recipient of Countryside Commission grant funding anywhere in Britain. This was because we completed our projects at a speed which allowed it to hold us up as an example of what could be achieved. The support of the Commission was crucial, but it was able to fund only up to a maximum of 50 per cent of our eligible expenditure. While many gardens got into difficulties raising the matched funding necessary to carry out their restoration work, we built on our reputation for the reliable handling of public and private financial resources. The key that unlocked the grant funding was our ability to match public funds with the generosity of the many volunteers who donated their time in lieu of money, and with the largesse of our sponsors. Their willingness to help us was, in part, a direct result of the deepest recession in recent memory. To put it simply, many talented people were temporarily unemployed and had time on their hands, while many of the companies that assisted us did so because they had staff and equipment lying idle. To some extent it was a case of 'right time, right place', and the recipe for success was beyond our control. However, to date sixty-three companies have sponsored the work at Heligan, and we are in the fortunate position of having others waiting in the wings to contribute to work that isn't yet on stream.

It would be false modesty to claim that it has all been down to luck. While corporate sponsors needed to be persuaded of the mutual advantages of their involvement with the project, basically companies are only groups of people working together and if someone's interest could be engaged on a personal level, we were halfway there. The quantity and quality of Heligan's press coverage was an undoubted incentive to sponsors, but in most cases the initial commitment to offer help came out of a simple enthusiasm for the adventure of it all. The rationale was usually worked out afterwards. We have continued to nurture these relationships and many of our sponsors have remained good friends of the project.

While we have been extremely fortunate in the grant funding we have received, a point that is often missed is that grants, properly used, are not free gifts. Their purpose is to prime the pumps. The Task Force Trees initiative has now drawn to a close. From it we have received in the order of £500,000 in grant aid, but, in the five years that we have been open to the public, we have paid more than twice that amount to Customs and Excise in VAT, and to the Inland Revenue in corporation tax, PAYE and National Insurance contributions. If you add to that the contribution made by keeping fifty people in work, many of whom were previously unemployed and a drain on the exchequer, you begin to see the dynamic nature of properly applied grant funding.

The restoration of Heligan has had a futher impact on the local economy. Cornwall's visitor season has traditionally concentrated on the main summer holiday period, which has resulted in harshly seasonal employment. At Heligan we have encouraged year-round visiting and as a result are busy from the third week in February right through to the end of the first week in November. The dramatic impact on local hotels and services has permeated throughout the local community, as more and more jobs become permanent. It is rewarding to be able to give something back to those who were our staunchest supporters from the start.

And so, as many say in jest, the 'lost' gardens have been well and truly found. Literature about the restoration travels to the four corners of the earth and brown road signs direct tourists from St Austell. The recognition of our achievement has given us the opportunity to advise others working on similar projects, and to participate in outside affairs. Heligan now offers an environment for serious learning on a number of levels. But ultimately if you can't make love in it, dream or be merry in it, what is the point of having it?

A garden is one of the ultimate human conceits, living architecture, perverting the course of nature to human ends. Leave it for a moment and the conceit is revealed for what it is, as the land reverts to nature's rhythm and imperatives. A gardener is merely putting off the inevitable encroachment of the wild. It is in this that I can sense the real hold that gardens and gardening have on the imagination, with the inexorable rolling pageant of the seasons and all the attendant triumphs and disasters at the hands of nature. The relativity and transience of each success encourages humility.

The tragedy of our human condition is that we do not truly appreciate what we have, until we have lost it. At Heligan, we have a second chance.

Part Four

THE FINAL ACT

Chapter 16

SPIRIT OF HELIGAN

November in Cornwall is a bleak, dark month. Nobody chooses to be here. The autumn gales have stripped the deciduous trees of their greenery and typically endless rain reduces the ground to a quagmire. There is little striking autumn colour and most of the nuts and berries have already been hoarded. The few blooms left in the garden flower only half-heartedly – the odd chrysanthemum, fuchsia, cyclamen or an unseasonal campion. And yet, if you stop and look again, all the promise of another season is starting to unfold. The buds on the 'Christmas camellia' at the top of the main ride are beginning to swell and, fingers crossed, after a few days indoors some chosen stems will flower for the festive season.

Into the new year, every day is met with excitement, as the Jungle floor becomes a carpet of snowdrops, and the camellia collection presents a new and perfect treasure with each week that passes. By mid-February there is considerable colour in the garden, with early daffodils starting to fill bare patches on the ground, and some of the rhododendron buds beginning to break, offering a streak of pink or red or white. If the often bitter March winds don't steal them, the huge pink blossoms of the *Magnolia campbellii* will be visible from the other side of Pentewan, and for Easter, whenever it falls, there will be primroses in the hedgerows. In a good year, an almost overwhelming display of huge, old, flowering shrubs hijacks most of the Northern Gardens, and the blooms of the infamous rampant laurel release their fragile scent. Meanwhile, the woodland path to the Jungle winds through a sea of bluebells, seen through sunlight dappled by the tender new foliage of the massive beeches. The sub-tropical valley seethes with new life, the singing yellow of the fresh skunk cabbage drawing the eye to the swamp to witness the regeneration of the giant gunnera. The smell of wild garlic fills the air and everywhere, from within the high nests of the ancient tree ferns to the tiniest crevices between the rocks, the furry fronds of ferns uncurl. Violets, wood anemones, comfrey, stitchwort, bugloss and, of course, the luminous campion – all flower with renewed vigour, as spring turns to early summer and the foxgloves stand proud in every view. And then, as the bright crimsons fade for another season and the drifts of rhododendron petals smother the surface of the top lake, the marvellous high drama of nature is balanced by the orderliness of the earliest cropping, up in the productive gardens.

There are eyes skinned for the first strawberries of the season, asparagus, early salads and new potatoes. Within the sun-baked walls of the Flower Garden, especially tender vegetables might be ready for gathering in May or June, and with every week that passes thereafter, separate little plots within the box hedging are harvested and replanted. There is a constant cycle of renewal. Out in the Vegetable Garden, the final rows of curiously named and fantastically coloured old potato varieties are lifted, to make way for the brassica seedlings, which will need a good strewing of fresh seaweed to keep the pests at bay. While the first pea pods are gathered, the runner beans create a wall of colour with their bright flowers, and the soft fruits – the many currants, gooseberries and raspberries – fill punnet after punnet. The height of summer is evoked by the breathtaking array of Victorian flowers, grown, yes, especially for picking; row upon row upon row along the length of the vinery, viewed from every possible angle to make sure the sight is not a snapshot sent from heaven. I shall always remember the experience of that first, ripe, home-grown peach meeting my lips, and its sweet juice pouring sinfully down my neck …

And then, while summer's joys begin to fade away, there is more to look forward to, as the pumpkins swell on the ground beside the path and an array of multi-coloured, oddly shaped squashes emerges from the dying foliage. There are little melons, lifted carefully from their net bags, and in the years to come, there will be grapes to cut from the new vines. Winter soups made from freshly dug leeks, or artichokes selected from the clamp in the dark room, will meet our need for seasonally warm nourishment, and the fantastic choice of weirdly unpromising-looking root crops will add variety and flavour to both stews and roast dishes, as we try to console ourselves in the face of the shortening daylight hours and the onset of winter once again.

There is an inevitable symmetry in the march of the seasons, mirrored by the changeless pattern of the garden year. Those who once worked here, whose story we sought to tell, what have we learned of them? Or do we know them only through ourselves? How unexpected it is to have embarked on the restoration of a garden, a voyage into history, full of adventure, and to find that the restoration itself has become a story within the story. What of the past? We can feel and hear its distant heartbeat, as if it were our own. The restoration has breathed life into the old framework, and with that new life, with that strengthening pulse, has picked up the rhythm of the seasons once again. And as the garden returns to garden and the land is in good heart once more, you realize that the story we wished to tell is there among us. For we are most surely no different from them.

As a winter sun broke over the Lost Valley, plumes of blue-grey smoke rose from the charcoal-burning kilns in the valley floor below me. In that smoke, I could see the shadows of men working, moving timber. The scene was almost medieval and matched the atmosphere of this extraordinary place. John was embarking on his greatest quest.

The screaming of the chainsaws had been stilled some days ago. Where once there had been a woodland of straggly trees set in a swamp, there now was a clearing, winding away as far as the eye could see. From my hillside eyrie, I could read the landscape like the body of a woman. Every curve and dimple, every nook and cranny, crag and crevice told a story. Revealed, for the first time in more than one hundred and fifty years, was what appeared to be the outline of two lakes, with their dams, and the leats that had once served the old mill further down the valley. There were quarries and charcoal-burning platforms, and avenues of beech and oak with here and there a grizzled sweet chestnut; their many limbs a testament to the once vigorous coppicing regime.

John and I had only recently understood the significance of this place. We had walked here often, but the woodland had hidden its secrets from us. Predominantly self-seeded ash and sycamore, none of it was more than a hundred years old. The old maps refer to it as Old Wood and we had assumed that the original wood had been felled as part of the home effort in the First World War, to be replaced by these pioneer species. It was only because John and I had wanted to find a suitable site to build a new garden – our own contribution to Heligan – that we had decided to take a closer look. When we traced the field boundaries across the bottom of the valley it became apparent that they were not what they seemed. They were enormous dams.

Over Christmas 1995, a BTCV working group had arrived for a fortnight of unremitting punishment – clearing the valley floor of weed trees and brash. Joined by our chainsaw team, the speed of their work was an inspiration as the original landscape unfolded before us, and the roar of swollen underground streams added to the sense of danger and exhilaration out on our new frontier. Through the winter our own staff continued the work of clearance further up the valley.

Then we called in the Cornwall Archaeological Unit to do a survey. They mapped the dams and gushing subterranean watercourses and pointed out various other features which indicated that the valley had evolved from a working wood-land, with a mill pond and possibly a stew pond (for fish), to the designed landscape of tree-lined gallops first recorded on the plan made by William Hole in 1777 for Henry Hawkins Tremayne. Some of the venerable oaks beside these routes are of even greater age than that. The strangest thing of all is that none of the plans or maps shows any sign of lakes and waterworks in this area, save for the mention of Heligan Mill.

John was recovering from eighteen months of discomfort, caused by a fall which had fractured his ribs, and he was like a hound on a scent. He was singularly focused on this latest challenge. The archaeologists were followed by the site surveyors who in turn gave way to the Silvanus Trust who carried out a tree survey. Dominic Cole, our landscape architect and garden historian, already a frequent visitor to Heligan, came down again from London and started developing an extension to the restoration plan, based on archival records and the recent field surveys. He and John paced around Old Wood, John pointing out the new discoveries and Dominic making sketches of vistas and tossing around ideas for the future. The outline of one lake was indisputable and John was convinced that there had been a second lake at the top of the valley. Dominic was less certain.

Finally, in the summer of 1996, with Vivianne breathing down his neck and demanding 'action', John took the decision to go ahead. A team of heavy horses was brought in to extract felled timber from the difficult and sensitive locations that couldn't be reached by machinery. We wanted to save as much good timber as we could for future use. The magnificent cob/shire crosses in their full livery were a beautiful and awesome sight as their handlers worked them in impossible terrain. Their big tufty hooves moved with a delicacy that belied their size, and their snorting good humour was a joy to watch as they proceeded up the steep side of the valley, ears pricked and eyes blinkered so as to keep their minds on the job in hand. In many cases they were pulling out whole trees. The lack of damage in the wake of these large and dignified animals was quite remarkable.

Over the next six weeks John orchestrated the transformation. The digger driver he booked for the excavations was no less sensitive to the landscape than the horses. He walked the valley for several hours, to understand its contours and establish reliable access causing the minimum of damage. Finally, his enormous earth moving machine breached the field walls and headed down to begin some breathtaking engineering work. As the first scoop was taken out, John leapt up and down like a gold prospector. There, in the cross-section, was the evidence he sought: layer upon layer of silt. He'd been right. There had been a second lake here.

Three thousand cubic metres of silt were then shifted and reabsorbed into the landscape lower down, to create a water meadow. Hundreds of tons of stone were extracted by the digger from one of the old quarries in the valley, and moved by dumper truck to rebuild the dams for both the lakes. The tree roots were carted out and the original gallops were cleared back to their full width. Then, with a salute from its giant bucket, the digger reversed out of the valley as stealthily as it had come, and there was silence.

Assisted by Dave Burns, Tiggy Duff, Barry Merritt and Mike Helliwell's enlarged team, John set to with a vengeance. Bridges were built, waterfalls were constructed, leats repaired and sluice gates installed. The raw scarred earth was dug over and prepared for planting. James Tancock, a new but resourceful student on site, was given the task of scouting out water plants for the new lakes, which by now were filling up fast, fed by the springs at Pengrugla and Peruppa. St Austell born and bred, James knew the area well and soon found some promising leads. The lakes at Charlestown, formerly used to sluice the harbour, were his first port of call, followed by an old lake belonging to English China Clays. Dozens of trips were made by the tractor and trailer team to bring back thousands of plants. The reeds and lilies were planted in their new home and John scattered grass seed all over the damaged areas to speed up the regeneration process. Once the water meadow was made ready for planting next spring, John finally started to relax.

If I close my eyes, I can recall the deathly stillness of my first visit to Heligan – and the complete absence of birdsong. Now, the constant chirruping, squawking and calling of many dozens of species provides the background music to each passing day. The restoration has encouraged an explosion of wildlife in the gardens, the only unwelcome guests being the rabbits, wood pigeons and grey squirrels sent to torment the staff in the Vegetable Garden, and the sparrow-hawk intent on using our new dovecote as a take-away service. The distinctive brown-faced badgers come and go from their huge sett above Old Wood and the foxes roam brazenly through the Jungle, as if they recognize it as a safe haven. In the deep woods there are frequent reports of an albino fox that flits like a ghost through the trees. There have been sightings, too, of mink, slow worms, grass snakes and adders and even the rumour of an otter. In early October 1996 the first ducks landed back on the new lakes in the Lost Valley, staked their claim and took up residence on the island with the wibbly-wobbly oak.

The flat land just south of the Jungle and adjacent to the new water meadow was also cleared in 1996, because John and I still had a plan. I had been inspired by an illustration from an eighteenth-century book which attempted to demonstrate that the Gothic style originated from the Teutonic forests. The author had sought to prove his point by building a church of living trees. I discussed the idea with John and he was as enthusiastic as I. We would build a living cathedral in the Byzantine style using trees such as willow, hazel, birch, chestnut and cypress for the bulk of the structure, and selecting specimen trees for the architectural features, with creepers of various sorts as stained-glass windows. If we cut a line through the woods to the west, the setting sun would light up the nave. A sylvan cathedral dedicated to nature will be our gift to the gardens.

A garden is never finished. Like Sisyphus, condemned for eternity to push a boulder to the top of the mountain, only for it to roll down just before the summit is reached, the gardener prefers to travel hopefully than to arrive. 'The trouble with getting there,' as Dorothy Parker once famously remarked, 'is that when you get there, there is no there, there.' My sentiments exactly.

Many parts of the estate remain to be uncovered, and yet others could be brought back into use in the future. The Long Drive which winds up from Pentewan is still in good condition although the avenues of exotics which once lined its route are now mostly gone, as are the apple orchards which covered the hillside at its highest point. The impenetrable Temple Woods above Mevagissey, which in their heyday contained miles of gallops, might be tackled one day. The eponymous Folly Temple, designed as a romantic ruin to be viewed from the comfort of Heligan House, could once again draw the gaze. We will find no shortage of challenges in the years to come.

People have lived at Heligan since prehistoric times. It is a stage set on which countless generations have played out their lives. My early research into the Tremayne family encouraged me to think of the estate in terms of ownership. Now I have a wider perspective and realize that we, the players, are but stewards passing through. To think otherwise is vanity. What makes gardening different – especially the intensive kind we practise at Heligan – is that one can never own anything. Gardening is an endless process, demanding active participation. Therein lies the reward.

If the garden is symbolic, like those journeys into the deep woods in the fairy tales of old, I see it as a metaphor for redemption and discovery. There are those who have come and gone and those who still remain, each with their own story, a strand in the Heligan tapestry. 'Heligan' – as one of our earliest and most devoted Friends, Douglas Holland, once observed – is an anagram of 'healing', and as I cast around among my friends and colleagues who have made the journey with me, I can see that in many cases healing forces have indeed been at work. Those who look for symbols and hidden meaning will always find them, for the astrologer pundits have a large and eager constituency in a world of uncertainty. My sympathies in general lie elsewhere, closer to the rationalism of Richard Dawkins, who would dismiss such irrational sentiment as being just that – irrational. But I must admit to wondering, in those quiet moments, in the seething silence of the Heligan night, if there is not something here that I may never understand.

As I write these final words and reflect with affection on the last few years, the wind is howling and the rain is pounding at the window. Our old farmhouse at Treveague is taking another battering. The huge chimney at the west end was rebuilt several years ago, and now stands full front to another Atlantic gale. I can hear intermittent dripping again and have spotted a fresh patch of damp on the ceiling. I shall have to call a builder in the morning.

Come to think of it, I know just the man.

Postscript

THE FRUITS OF OUR LABOURS

A heat haze dances above the enormous manure heap, piled high against the inside wall of the Melon Garden. Charles Fleming, Simon Lawday and Mike Rundle are forking it over in careful preparation for eventual decanting into the heating trenches of the pineapple pit, their clothes providing the only period marker for an otherwise timeless activity. Recently they have set about this loathsome and back-breaking task with a will, fired by their new boss's unwavering determination to secure the first fruiting of his most significant new charges.

The last couple of years have passed in a blur for those who work here. While the garden team embraces more and more of the early traditions of this place and we endeavour to maintain and enhance our achievement on the ground, Heligan's reputation has spread and attracted attention from all over the world. 1997 was, for us all, an *annus mirabilis*. In March John and I hosted the formal opening of the Lost Valley. Our pre-season annual party for hoteliers of the region was bolstered by hundreds of Friends of Heligan for this particularly special occasion. They all made their way, crocodile fashion, down into the valley below the Jungle and came to a halt by the old oak tree on the Georgian gallop, where a brightly coloured ribbon was strung across the path. We had invited Vivianne Howard, the director of the Channel 4 television documentary, to do the honours (with very blunt scissors). She had been with us from the beginning of this latest restoration project and had witnessed the valley's gradual return from dank overgrown swamp to designed landscape. The paths and lakesides, incongruously packed with people for this single event, still stood stark and bare, but the final shape of the place was there and the later adornment of spring colour was to complete the picture as we all had hoped. Assisted rather than impeded by man, nature still performs miracles. The Lost Valley now entices visitors to explore acres of new territory – a native woodland counterpoint to the exotic Jungle and the more formal Northern Gardens.

March 1997 also brought the first episode of the Channel 4 television series to our screens and saw the publication of this book. Both were enthusiastically received, and immediately thousands more people began to make their way to Heligan every week. We had already invited the Cornwall Garden Society to join us in hosting their centenary spring flower show in April, an event for which we had been preparing for many months. We were keen to put on a show which broke with the formal British tradition and reflected instead the more casual French style of a medieval tented village with lots to see and do, a crackle in the air and the babble of happy voices on the wind. A theatre group and musicians added to the fun, as it turned out, in gloriously unbroken spring sunshine and 27,000 people joined us for the three-day period of the Theatre of Flowers. The floral competition exhibits were as fine as anyone could remember. Each and every one of our team threw themselves wholeheartedly into their roles as hosts and were delighted, and totally exhausted, by the experience.

By coincidence, the day before the show started I received a phone call from a man in Dorchester who had been following the documentary series and, while browsing through a local auction catalogue, had come across a set of miniatures depicting a family named Tremayne. When he read out the list of names – Henry Hawkins and Mary Clotworthy, John Hearle and Henrietta and John Tremayne – I was left in no doubt that they were the Heligan Tremaynes. The following day, with the Theatre of Flowers in full swing, I retreated to my office for half an hour to bid for the collection over the telephone and secured the lot on Heligan's behalf. That day it felt as though we were finally pulling together all the strands of the project. The cream of the county's horticultural exhibits were on display, the gardens themselves looked superb, our staff were receiving the respect they so deserved and the Tremaynes of today were present and involved with it all. When John Nelson and I finally took possession of the portraits some weeks later, we both instinctively felt that they should be returned to their family and so we gave them to John and Katharine Willis, in safekeeping for their son James.

It's amazing what turns people on. Philip and Tom had been trying to fruit the pineapple plants for two years, without success, when Richard Dee took over responsibility for the productive gardens in the autumn of 1996. He was immediately intrigued by the problem. In no time at all he began a regime of regular measurements in the manure trenches of the pineapple pit, and spotted that huge variations in temperature were occurring. He decided to start again and devised his own layering technique with the manure until he was satisfied that he was in control. Like an expectant father he watched and waited. The air of expectation was so thick you could cut it. Surely we couldn't have propagated two hundred sterile plants? Then it happened. The news travelled like wildfire. A tiny red bud had formed at the centre of one of the pines. All the staff left their posts and made their way to the Melon Garden where, in the early May sunshine, Richard pulled back one of the beaver-tail lights to allow us a peek at his progeny.

At the beginning of June there were more plants in bud, so when HRH the Prince of Wales came to see us on a pre-arranged private visit, the pineapple pit became an obvious focus for his tour. A raised dais was built especially to enable him to look into the pit. Richard positioned himself inside it and held up one of his prize specimens for admiration as he described his work, his rich, full and sometimes earthy vocabulary held in check. He was dumbstruck when His Royal Highness responded with a remark about the amount of horseshit that must have been shovelled. Recovering rapidly and warming to the theme, Richard promised that a ripe pine would be sent on later as proof of success.

Lovingly nurtured, the buds turned to flowers and then to fruits, and by the middle of October the first ones were ripe. In front of a scrum of cameras and microphones Richard harvested a Jamaica Queen with a machete. Holding it aloft before his team, he declared that this first one should be sent to Her Majesty the Queen, at that time celebrating her Golden Wedding anniversary. Minutes later the doubts set in, prompted by a casual question as to whether we could be sure that the fruit would not taste of horse manure. It was hastily decided that the staff should try the first one just to check. John Nelson ceremonially cut it into strips and Philip McMillan Browse was accorded the honour of the first tasting. (After all, it was Philip who had set us on this course three years previously.) We waited in suspense. Finally he declared the flavour excellent – much to our, and I think his, surprise. Our first pineapple tasted superb; a fizzy combination of tart, juicy and sweet.

Number Two did go to Buckingham Palace, although it nearly didn't gain admittance. The police at the back gate thought the whole idea so unlikely that they insisted I unpack it before they would summon a lady-in-waiting. The fruit, the first of the ripe Cayennes, was packed in a cardboard box, nestling in a cradle of straw. The sight of policemen lifting it out and tapping and sniffing it, before finally agreeing that it was indeed a pineapple, will stay with me for some time. The Palace subsequently wrote a charming letter to Richard Dee thanking him for the pine and reporting that Her Majesty had enjoyed it for supper that night. Hence it was the third pine which eventually went to Prince Charles and the fourth to Tony Hibbert at Trebah Gardens, in celebration of his eightieth birthday. After that we decided to release just one more into the outside world, so we auctioned it off for charity – after all, these were possibly the most expensive pineapples ever known. At a rough estimate they had cost between £600 and £1,000 each to produce, although that wasn't really the point. So as not to devalue the experience, the rest of the crop was given to friends, including Peter Thoday and John Chamberlain who had helped Heligan along the way, and distributed among our staff. At the time of writing, Richard is bringing on the second generation, which should prove that his first effort wasn't just a case of beginner's luck.

The 1997 season yielded up further pleasures, as well as a disappointment. In the New Year Christian Lamb, an old friend of the gardens, had brought me a collection of seeds which had been found in her grandfather's attic in Scotland.

It was of named varieties of imported American melon, dating from the mid-nineteenth century. Each variety was wrapped in oiled paper and individually identified in beautiful copperplate writing. They were now no longer to be found in any of the catalogues, so we were excited by the possibility of bringing them back into production. Philip injected a note of caution. Melon seed, he warned me, kept notoriously badly and despite all his efforts not a single seed germinated. However, by the late summer, the restored melon house was none the less, for the first time, heavily laden with magnificent traditional varieties of melon, which Philip had sourced elsewhere. As they grew, they were strung in little nets, allowing them to ripen *in situ* before being harvested and greatly enjoyed.

Some years previously Philip had contacted a Mrs Maclean who had a famous collection of rare potato varieties which he wanted to try at Heligan. As is the way with collectors, she was extremely generous and had supplied us with a number of each of the varieties we sought. One of them was called Salad Blue, whose significant attribute is that the flesh is entirely blue, even after cooking. We grew them very successfully and over several years bulked them up. Then we heard that Mrs Maclean's 1997 crop of Salad Blues had failed and we were delighted to be able to return the compliment. Generosity in the garden world is an essential ingredient of survival. To have all supplies in one ownership is far too much of a responsibility for any of us to carry.

Cornwall's climate is generally too mild to trigger stunning autumn colour in the woodland, but this particular year it more than compensated in the productive gardens. The rows of pom-pom chrysanthemums which lined the arched pathway through the Vegetable Garden developed into hedges of blazing and long-lasting colour. In the Flower

Garden we cropped a tremendous range and quantity of fine squashes – enough to make splendid displays at Harvest Festival celebrations throughout all three local parishes. Meanwhile the new vines in the vinery made their first few meagre offerings, the ultimate symbol of resurgence and the dawn of a new productive era for Heligan.

After such an extraordinary year we should have expected that something would go wrong – in the event, we entered a period of meteorological high drama. In the late autumn the immediate vicinity of Heligan was suddenly struck by flash flooding. The White River in the Pentewan valley burst its banks and flooded two villages. A local garage disappeared under six feet of water and terraces of houses filled with mud. For much of the way back to St Austell the road was submerged and bridges and walls were washed away. The devastation occurred in a matter of hours while most people were at work. There was no means of getting on or off the peninsula and many of our staff were marooned at Heligan, unable to return home until the floodwaters subsided. After a reconnaissance of the Lost Valley, Dave Burns reported with alarm that both of the new lakes were flooding their dams, even with the sluice gates open. John was extremely concerned by the prospect of hundreds of thousands of gallons of water carrying all before it, through Heligan Mill and down to Mevagissey. However, there was absolutely nothing anyone could do to stop the surge, except drink hot toddies and hope. While the gardens eventually pulled through, waterlogged but unscathed, the homes and cars of some of the staff disappeared under several feet of water, resulting in major damage.

In December Heligan had a heavy fall of snow, followed in the New Year by hurricane-force winds again. It was now that our heavy investment in an extensive tree surgery and replanting programme over the last six years reaped dividends. While there was widespread destruction throughout Cornwall, Heligan withstood the elements, losing only one large ash tree which toppled into the Mill Pool in the Lost Valley.

After Easter 1998, it snowed again. On Flora's Green we were presented with an extraordinary tableau of rhododendrons and camellias in full flower, against a pure white canvas. And then came more serious rain. April 1998 was to be the wettest since records began. Towards the end of the month we were to host the second Theatre of Flowers and expected thousands of visitors. No one will ever forget this show either. The staff had to work round the clock for weeks beforehand to meet the challenge of the weather. In places, where vehicles had entered the show site, an impenetrable quagmire was developing. We pulled favours from all our friends and brought in hundreds of tons of hardcore, followed by truckloads of woodchips, in order to present an unruffled face as the first show day broke (dry, would you believe?). It is at times like this that you realize why Heligan is so special. The team refused to accept a situation which, anywhere else I know, would have meant the cancellation of the show.

The wettest April was followed by the second wettest May and June, and the expected volume of visitors simply didn't come to Cornwall. This provided us with a salutary lesson on the fundamental economic difference between Heligan past and Heligan present. We are totally dependent on visitors. They were not. However, the visitors who did come during 1998 were treated to the most stunning lushness in the Jungle since the restoration's inception. The tree ferns and the bamboos burgeoned thanks to an absence of frost the previous winter, the swamp plants thrived in the extremely damp conditions, and in the confusion the early- and late-flowering rhododendrons dramatically all bloomed together.

In the productive gardens the lack of sunshine retarded the onset of summer colour and the team faced a new round of horticultural challenges. Not altogether surprisingly, the weather and our continuing desire to garden organically led to a blighted potato crop, and all our potato stocks will probably need to be replaced for next season. Once again it will be our turn to look to Mrs Maclean and other collectors to help us rebuild our supplies of rare varieties and protect them for the future.

However, our herbaceous border in the Sundial Garden was at last living up to its potential, despite the best efforts of an army of slugs and voracious rabbits. Lander King, who had arrived to take responsibility for the Northern Gardens on Annabel's departure, had used his expertise with grass to bring a stripe to the lawn and a smile to all our faces, before joining John to embark on the development of the gardens surrounding the Northern Summerhouse. The present-day challenge in both these small areas of the Pleasure Grounds is to construct individual and attractive gardens which can thrive, notwithstanding the passage of thousands of feet. Outside the Northern Summerhouse the tatty patch of grass has been replaced with a paving of huge slates, hauled up from the old dog kennels, which can now be viewed through our first attempt to cut windows back into the new boundary hedge.

For the best part of a year the Heligan team, led by John Nelson, worked with the design company LWL to create an exhibit for the 1998 Hampton Court Palace Flower Show entitled 'Spirit of Heligan'. The stand would recreate the walls of the Flower Garden and feature, on one side, a vista of dereliction with an old gutted greenhouse replete with rusty ironwork and broken glass, smothered in ferns and bramble. The centrepiece would be a replica of the old wooden door, which, half ajar, would allow glimpses through to the restored garden with its neat rows of vegetables and espaliered fruit. Behind it would be a collage of features from the Pleasure Grounds including the Wishing Well and the rockery that leads to the Crystal Grotto. It was a thought-provoking experience to watch the Heligan team operate on two levels: in Cornwall, continuing to restore the past; in London, recreating its present with reference to its past. While everyone was delighted to be awarded a Gold Medal for the stand, further pursuit of such imagery would, I feel, be retrograde and pandering to the sort of romantic nostalgia we hate.

In its advertising for the Hampton Court Show, the RHS magazine described the Lost Gardens of Heligan as 'leading a current trend'. Most of the media attention has been welcome, but the public obsession with nostalgia has raised some uncomfortable questions for the future of Heligan as a time capsule reflecting the spirit of an age which has passed.

How, for instance, can you tell the story with integrity when the social structures which created and fuelled the estate are long gone? Is the harsh truth that Heligan has become an experience like many others, peddling romantic dreams to its visitors; who, while they may spend many agreeable hours in a misty-eyed reverie for a past that was never quite as they imagine, will leave entertained but unchallenged?

On reflection I have come to two conclusions about this. First, many of the people who are attracted to Heligan, and I include myself among them, do retain a romantic attachment to particular experiences in their childhood. But adults, on returning to the scenes of their earliest memories, are often disappointed by them. The reality seems so much smaller and less mysterious than what we remember. Heligan, with its characteristic Peter Rabbit-style productive gardens, is nevertheless on such a scale that it does not disappoint; instead it satisfies something deep within us. It is ironic that part of Heligan's appeal should be attributable to its living up to something that never existed in the first place. Rather than nurturing false visions of an idyllic past, what we are trying to do is to tell the real story of the ordinary men and women who once worked here, and this is a tradition with which a number of our visitors are familiar, either at first or second hand.

Second, the Lost Gardens of Heligan is an evocative name which could become little more than a marketing puff now that the gardens have been 'found'. However, Heligan's importance to me lies not in its faithful recreation of the past, but in the relevance of its past to the future. An issue that confronts all who work with heritage of any kind is that once a period becomes history, its visible remains become little more than monuments, leaving us, the inheritors, to interpret them from the perspective of our own time. Heligan treasures the physical remains of its past, but lays a heavy emphasis on exploring old working methods and approaches to horticulture to discover where they can make a contribution to improving modern practices. The fruits of our labours are real enough for all to see, but the restoration and the way of life to which it alludes may have substance only for as long as the public can be diverted to appreciate it. Popularity is a fickle mistress and while we acknowledge that Heligan is 'leading a current trend', we want people to understand that it is down a path of a more serious nature that we wish to proceed.

It is important that we question modern-day practices in mass food production and their effects on biodiversity. We need to recognize the degree of our dependence on plants. The loss of many varieties noted for their excellent flavour and amenable cropping characteristics is only one sad result of applying market forces. In simple terms, Heligan wants to protect that which is good about the past, those crops and methods of husbandry that have truly stood the test of time, and thus should have a role to play in the future. If we succeed, the Lost Gardens will become less an evocative description of place than a living celebration of a relevant and valuable tradition under threat. Moreover, it is a subject unconfined by the narrow boundaries of a small estate in Cornwall; but therein lies another story.

Special Note to the Third Edition

In a few weeks it will be a decade since I first set foot in the Lost Gardens. My good friend and partner at Heligan, John Nelson, has just decided to park up his famous 'iron horse'. In fact, tonight is his retirement party. The time has come to leave others to enjoy the pleasures of the fierce easterly wind and the damp that gets into the marrow through layers of weatherproof clothing. It's a job for a younger man, he says. In all this time he has only taken a week off and, as I recall, Christmas Days.

Actually, John and his wife Lyn have recently travelled to Vancouver Island where he delivered a talk on our work at Heligan and he's finally rumbled me – it's fun. After years of critically judging the work on the ground that still needed to be done it made a refreshing break to celebrate what had been achieved so far. So, having got a taste for it, he's off to New Zealand and Australia on a lecture tour in March 2000. He has decided to progress into an ambassadorial role, as a sort of dissolute elder statesman with a twinkle in the eye. It is ironic that he will be taking tales of buried treasure and strange goings on in the Jungle back to the countries from which many of the glories of Heligan emerged in the first place. The Heligan story will, in effect, be going full circle.

Good luck, mate.

Tim Smit
3 December 1999

Picture Acknowledgements

In our early days at Heligan no one could have foreseen that a full restoration of the gardens would be possible, or of interest to the outside world, so we are extremely fortunate that a number of the people who visited the site at that time kept a photographic record of discoveries. We are also fortunate in our friend Herbie Knott, who came down in 1991 while working for the *Independent* and, under duress, shot a couple of films in the depths of the dereliction. These have since proved invaluable.

As the project gathered momentum, it not only attracted professional photographers seeking 'set piece' shots for commissions from colour magazines, but also prompted the idea of recording, pictorially, a diary of our progress. Local photographer David Hastilow has been on call since 1993 and it is his photographs that have enabled us to illustrate the course of the restoration in such depth.

Claire Travers was commissioned more recently with a view to capturing the 'flowers and faces' of Heligan. Early in 1997 Charles Francis moved in to one of the old farm buildings on the estate, and we have since been lucky enough to have the restoration recorded on an almost daily basis.

We are particularly grateful to those who have agreed to allow old black and white photographs to be published, and to the one or two whose pictures appear uncredited because we could not track them down. We hope they will be proud to see their work in print.

Photographers

Dave Burns (DB)
Derek Cattani (DC)
Charles Francis (CF)
Ferdinand Graf Luckner (FGL)
David Hastilow (DH)
Colin Howlett (CH)
Julia Husband (JH)
Ian Jackson (IJ)
Andrea Jones (AJ)

Herbie Knott (HK)
Marie O'Hara (MO'H)
Hugh Palmer (HP)
Sue Pring (SP)
Dawn Runnals (DR)
Candy Smit (CS)
Tim Smit (TS)
Claire Travers (CT)

Picture Credits

THE LOST GARDENS OF HELIGAN

SECTION 3		SECTION 4	
Page	Photographer	Page	Photographer
1	courtesy Commission–Air	1	top DH
2	top DH		bottom AJ
	bottom HP	2	top left & right & bottom DH
3	top CS	3	top HK
	bottom DH		bottom CF
4	HK	4	top CF
5	top HK		bottom DH
	middle MO'H	5	top courtesy Penelope Willis
	bottom AJ		middle JH
6	top DH		bottom DH
	middle CF	6	CS
	bottom CF/courtesy Duchy of Cornwall	7	top right CT
			bottom DH
7	CF	8	DH
8	top HK	9	AJ
	bottom DH	10	top CF
9	top MO'H		bottom DR
	bottom CS	11	IJ/courtesy Western Morning News
10	top left & right FGL	12	CH
	bottom left AJ		
	bottom right FGL		
11	AJ		
12	DH		

Front cover   HK
Inside front cover   donated by Tab Anstice
Maps (text pp xviii-xix, xxi & xxiii)   drawn by Sue Pring
Page 139   Cross-section of the Pineapple Pit drawn by John Chamberlain ARIBA